Sehnsucht: The C. S. Lewis Journal

Sehnsucht: The C. S. Lewis Journal
Volume 16, 2022

General Editor
Bruce R. Johnson, *Mountain View Presbyterian Church,* Scottsdale, Arizona

Managing Editor
Jason Lepojärvi, *George Fox University,* Newberg, Oregon

Associate Editors
Joel D. Heck, *Concordia University,* Austin, Texas
James P. Helfers, *Grand Canyon University,* Phoenix, Arizona
Louis Markos, *Houston Baptist University,* Houston, Texas
Gary Tandy, *George Fox University,* Newberg, Oregon

Assistant Editors
William Gentrup, *Arizona State University,* Tempe, Arizona
Megan Novello, *University of Arizona,* Tucson, Arizona

Reviews Editor
Crystal Hurd
Northwind Seminary
Winter Garden, Florida

Poetry Editor
Brooks Lampe
George Fox University
Newberg, Oregon

Advisory Board

Grayson Carter
Fuller Theological Seminary
Phoenix, Arizona

Michael Ward
University of Oxford
Oxford, England

Diane Pavlac Glyer
Azusa Pacific University
Azusa, California

Inquiries and Subscriptions

The Arizona C. S. Lewis Society
Bruce R. Johnson, President

c/o Mountain View Presbyterian Church
8050 E. Mountain View Road
Scottsdale, Arizona 85258

Telephone: (480) 998-1085

Typesetting
William Gentrup
Tempe, Arizona

Society Treasurer
Jane Cicinelli
Scottsdale, Arizona

ISSN: 1940-5537
ISBNs: 978-1-6667-7059-9 (pbk); 978-1-6667-7060-5 (hdbk); 978-1-6667-7061-2 (e-book)

See back of this volume for submission details, copyright, and subscription form.

Published by Wipf and Stock Publishers, 199 West 8th Avenue, Eugene OR, 97401
www.wipfandstock.com. All rights reserved.

www.georgefox.edu/sehnsucht

Contents

Contributors   7

General Editor's Note
    Bruce R. Johnson   11

Articles

Which Image Triggered C. S. Lewis's Enthusiasm for Wagner's *Ring* cycle?
    Norbert Feinendegen   15

The Reading Life of Young Jack Lewis, 1914-1917
    Harry Lee Poe   23

Three University College Tutors: Arthur Blackburne Poynton, E. F. Carritt, and George Hope Stevenson
    Joel D. Heck   37

C. S. Lewis and The Personal Opinion Fallacy
    Jason Lepojärvi   73

C. S. Lewis and the Historical Imagination
    Jamin Metcalf and K. Alan Snyder   94

Poetry

Under a Bridge Downtown
    CHRIS JENSEN   113

When Dreams Die
    CHRIS JENSEN   114

The Verge
    J. ALEKSANDR WOOTTON   116

Book Reviews

Jason M. Baxter, *The Medieval Mind of C. S. Lewis: How Great Books Shaped a Great Mind*
    WILLIAM GENTRUP   120

P. H. Brazier, *A Hebraic Inkling: C. S. Lewis on Judaism and the Jews*
    ERIN SEIDEL   124

James Como, *Mystical Perelandra: My Lifelong Reading of C. S. Lewis and His Favorite Book*
    CRYSTAL HURD   127

Paul S. Fiddes, *Charles Williams and C. S. Lewis: Friends in Co-inherence*
    ANDREW LAZO   129

Peter Grybauskas, *A Sense of Tales Untold: Exploring the Edges of Tolkien's Literary Canvas*
    LAUREN SPOHN   131

Joel D. Heck, *No Ordinary People: Twenty-One Friendships of C. S. Lewis*
    JOSIAH PETERSON   135

Crystal Hurd, *The Leadership of C. S. Lewis:*
Ten Traits to Encourage Change and Growth
    JON HEERINGA   137

Bruce R. Johnson, ed., *The Undiscovered C. S. Lewis:*
Essays in Memory of Christopher W. Mitchell
    BRIAN C. RODEN   139

Joseph A. Kohm Jr., *The Unknown Garden*
of Another's Heart: The Surprising Friendship
between C. S. Lewis and Arthur Greeves
    JASON LEPOJÄRVI   141

Louis Markos, *C. S. Lewis for Beginners*
    BRUCE R. JOHNSON   144

John Rosegrant, *Tolkien, Enchantment, and Loss:*
Steps on the Developmental Journey
    JESSICA F. LEE   146

Harry Lee Poe, *The Completion of C. S. Lewis:*
From War to Joy (1945-1963)
    CRYSTAL HURD   148

Jim Prothero, *Sunbeams and Bottles:*
The Theology, Thought, and Reading of C. S. Lewis
    CHARLIE W. STARR   150

Film Review

The Most Reluctant Convert
    JAMES A. MOTTER   155

Theatre Review

The Lion, the Witch, and the Wardrobe
    SARAH WATERS   158

Miscellaneous

Submission Guidelines   165

Style Guide   167

Copyright   175

Subscription Form   177

Contributors

Norbert Feinendegen (Ph.D., University of Bonn), worked for several years as a research assistant at the Theological Faculty of the University of Bonn and is a freelance author and lecturer in the field of religious education for the Archdiocese of Cologne. He is the author of three German books and several essays about C. S. Lewis (in German and English) and has published with Arend Smilde *The 'Great War' of Owen Barfield and C. S. Lewis Philosophical Writings 1927-1930* (2015) and *C.S. Lewis: Tutor and Lecturer in Philosophy: Philosophical Notes, 1924* (2021). Feinendegen is currently preparing an updated version of his Ph.D. thesis *Denk-Weg zu Christus. C. S. Lewis als kritischer Denker der Moderne* (2008) for publication in English. He is advisor to the Owen Barfield Literary Estate and was a long-time board member of the German Inklings Society. His academic work focuses on the philosophy of C. S. Lewis, Christian apologetics, ethics and the relation of faith and science.

Joel D. Heck (Th.D., Concordia Seminary) is Assisting Pastor at Redeemer Lutheran Church. He has written extensively on C. S. Lewis, including *Irrigating Deserts: C. S. Lewis on Education* (2005). *From Atheism to Christianity: The Story of C. S. Lewis* (2017), *No Ordinary People: Twenty-One Friendships of C. S. Lewis* (2021), and *The Lion That Roared* (co-authored with his daughter Brenda Nauss, 2023). He has edited an edition of *The Personal Heresy: A Controversy* (2008), and *Socratic Digest* (2012). He has also written forty articles on C. S. Lewis, including two forthcoming articles, one on Albert Lewis and one on three of Lewis's Oxford tutors: Poynton, Carritt, and Stevenson (in this volume). He has created the well-known historical resource "Chronologically Lewis" on the lives of C. S. Lewis and his brother Warren, which he maintains at his website, www.joelheck.com.

Jason Lepojärvi (Ph.D., University of Helsinki) is the C. S. Lewis Associate Professor of Theology and Literature at George Fox University, Oregon, where he teaches in the Great Books Honors Program and directs the C. S. Lewis Initiative. A former president of the Oxford University C. S. Lewis Society, since 2023 Lepojärvi (pronounced Leh-poh-yar-ve) has served as the Managing Editor of *Sehnsucht: The C. S. Lewis Journal*. His writings on C. S. Lewis and J. R. R. Tolkien include his doctoral dissertation *God Is Love, but Love Is Not God: Studies on C. S. Lewis's Theology of Love* (2015) and various articles in *The Harvard Theological Review, Politics and Religion*, and *Religious Studies*.

Jamin Metcalf (M.H., University of Dallas) is a pastor, educator, and the Dean of Students at Chandler Preparatory Academy in Chandler Arizona, where he also teaches courses on Rhetoric, Ancient History, and American Literature. His is the author of *Why Christian Pedagogy Matters* (2019), *An Introduction to Ezekiel Workbook* (2016), and the original musical, *The Brightest Star* (2021).

Harry Lee Poe (Ph.D., Southern Baptist Theological Seminary) serves as Charles Colson Professor of Faith and Culture at Union University in Jackson, Tennessee. He has published five books related to C. S. Lewis: *Becoming C. S. Lewis, The Making of C. S. Lewis, The Completion of C. S. Lewis, The Inklings of Oxford*, and *C. S. Lewis Remembered*. The author of over a dozen articles and chapters on Lewis, he is a frequent speaker on Lewis at conferences, universities, libraries, and churches. Former board member and program director of the C. S. Lewis Foundation, Poe began the Inklings Fellowship in 2001, which conducts the annual Christianity in the Academy Conference, the annual Inklings Weekend in Montreat, and the triennial Inklings Week in Oxford. He is the author of fifteen other books on the intersection of the gospel and culture.

K. Alan Snyder (Ph.D., American University) has been a professor of history at four Christian universities over the last thirty-three years and is the author of five books, his latest being *America Discovers C. S. Lewis: His Profound Impact* (2016). Dr. Snyder continues to teach at Southeastern University in Lakeland, Florida as an adjunct professor of history and is on the staff of All Saints' Episcopal Church in Lakeland as developer and teacher of adult education classes. At All Saints' he has taught classes on *The Screwtape Letters*, *Mere Christianity*, the Chronicles of Narnia, and the Ransom Trilogy.

General Editor's Note

For the last six years, *Sehnsucht: The C. S. Lewis Journal* has been in search of a new academic home following the reorganization of Fuller Theological Seminary's Arizona campus. That search reached a positive conclusion in the fall of 2022 when the President of George Fox University, Dr. Robin Baker, approved a collaborative arrangement between the journal and the university. Our hope is that this will help ensure the continuation of *Sehnsucht*, and new academic work on C. S. Lewis, for many years to come.

Previously unpublished letters by C. S. Lewis, his brother Warren H. Lewis, and his wife Joy Davidman all appeared in the pages of last year's Volume 15. The speculation offered in the last General Editor's Note suggested that these new documents could encourage the appearance of "a supplemental volume 4 to *The Collected Letters of C. S. Lewis*." Something like that has begun to occur. The C. S. Lewis Correspondence Project will be to be formally announced in the coming months. Its goal is to provide digital access to the correspondence of C. S. Lewis with the initial priority on all his letters which did not find their way into the three volumes of *Collected Letters*. I am grateful for the small role *Sehnsucht* has played in the launch of this ongoing enterprise.

The change in academic affiliation has been accompanied by a reorganization of our Editorial Body. Associate Editor Arend Smilde has resigned in order to dedicate more of his time to the C. S. Lewis Correspondence Project. Poetry Editor Randall VanderMey has retired from his academic position and retired from his role at *Sehnsucht*. Additionally, our Editorial Advisory Board has been significantly reduced in size. Departing this year are James T. Como, Lyle W. Dorsett, Robert K. Johnston, Stanley Mattson, and Jerry Root. A great debt is owed to all these scholars for their faithful years of service to the journal.

Three George Fox University faculty members have joined our Editorial Body. Brooks Lampe becomes the fourth person appointed Poetry Editor of *Sehnsucht* and follows in the footsteps of Brett Foster, Scott Cairns, and Randall VanderMey. Jason Lepojärvi will serve in the role of Managing Editor, overseeing the transfer of certain operational aspects of the journal from Arizona to Oregon. Gary Tandy comes aboard as the new Associate Editor serving alongside of our continuing Associate Editors Joel Heck, James P. Helfers, and Louis Markos

The efforts of the entire Editorial Body are significant, and I remain grateful for what each editor contributes as well as for the labors of each author. As always, *Sehnsucht* remains committed to the collaborative goal of upholding the highest of academic standards while fostering new work on the life and writings of C. S. Lewis.

Bruce R. Johnson
December 2022
St. Lucia's Day

Articles

Which Image Triggered C. S. Lewis's Enthusiasm for Wagner's Ring Cycle?

NORBERT FEINENDEGEN

In his autobiography *Surprised by Joy*, C. S. Lewis recounts a seminal moment that occurred quite early in his life but had an enormous impact on his spiritual development. This encounter of art and imagination has become famous, and yet the image at the center of the story has remained a mystery.[1] Between January 1911 and July 1913, Lewis was educated at Cherbourg House, Malvern, a preparatory school southwest of Birmingham, England. At some point during these two and a half years, his eyes happened to fall on an advertisement in a literary magazine that promoted volume 2 of Arthur Rackham's illustrations of Richard Wagner's *Ring des Nibelungen* cycle.[2] He saw one of Rackham's paintings and at the same time read the words *Siegfried and The Twilight of the Gods*. This triggered an intense experience of Joy—the first since his childhood days— and established his lifelong fascination with Norse mythology.

Lewis gives two accounts of the event. The first is the well-known

---

[1] A slightly different version of this essay was published in April 2022 on Brenton Dickieson's *A Pilgrim in Narnia* blog. https://apilgriminnarnia.com/2022/04/20/wagner.

[2] Rackham's illustrations of *Siegfried and The Twilight of the Gods* were published in late October 1911, together with Margaret Armour's recent translation. https://archive.org/details/siegfriedtwiligh00wagn/mode/2up. Accessed 7 January 2023. The first volume, *The Rhinegold and The Valkyrie*, was published in 1910. Richard Wagner, *The Rhinegold and The Valkyrie*, trans. by Margaret Armour, illus. by Arthur Rackham (London: Heinemann, 1910); Richard Wagner, *Siegfried and the Twilight of the* Gods, trans. by Margaret Armour, illus. by Arthur Rackham (London: Heinemann, 1911).

passage in Chapter 5 "Renaissance" of *Surprised by Joy*:

> This long winter broke up in a single moment, fairly early in my time at Chartres. . . . Someone must have left in the schoolroom a literary periodical: The *Bookman*, perhaps, or the *Times Literary Supplement*. My eye fell upon a headline and a picture, carelessly, expecting nothing. A moment later, as the poet says, 'The sky had turned round.'
>
> What I had read was the words *Siegfried and the Twilight of the Gods*. What I had seen was one of Arthur Rackham's illustrations to that volume. I had never heard of Wagner, nor of Siegfried. I thought the Twilight of the Gods meant the twilight in which the gods lived. How did I know, at once and beyond question, that this was no Celtic, or silvan, or terrestrial twilight? But so it was. Pure 'Northernness' engulfed me: a vision of huge, clear spaces hanging above the Atlantic in the endless twilight of Northern summer, remoteness, severity … and almost at the same moment I knew that I had met this before, long, long ago (it hardly seems longer now) in *Tegner's Drapa*, that Siegfried (whatever it might be) belonged to the same world as Balder and the sunward-sailing cranes.[3]

The second account is a passage in "Early Prose Joy," an autobiographical sketch Lewis wrote in late 1930/early 1931:

> For two school years of busy and unprofitable boyhood, nothing befell me that concerns the subject of this book. Then all in a moment the frost broke up. I saw one day in a newspaper the reproduction of some picture that Arthur Rackham had drawn for Wagner's *Ring*. I suppose that what I was looking at must have been a publisher's advertisement, for my eyes, at the same moment, took in the words *Siegfried and The Twilight of the Gods* printed close beside the picture. I had never heard of Wagner, nor of Siegfried: and I thought that 'the twilight of the gods' meant the twilight in which the gods lived. It is a little remarkable that though I knew nothing of the Northern mythology till then, save what could be learned from Longfellow, I spontaneously set this twilight and these gods in a place quite apart either from the Celtic or from the Grecian stories. Perhaps the flavour of Rackham's drawings is truly Germanic and guided me aright. Whatever the cause, those printed words flashed instantly upon

---

[3] C. S. Lewis, *Surprised by Joy: The Shape of My Early Life* (New York: Harcourt, Brace and World, 1955), 72-3.

my mind a riot of imagery which later knowledge has shown to be surprisingly correct. I saw that twilight hanging pale and motionless over the Atlantic, slowly fading through the endless summer evening of the North: I saw those gods wheeling through it aloft on flying horses: I think (but of this I am uncertain) [that] even then, from some forgotten source, I supplied them with winged helmets.[4]

Lewis does not say in these two passages which of Rackham's illustrations he saw, but he assumes in *Surprised by Joy* that the advertisement appeared in *The Bookman* or *The Times Literary Supplement*. In both *Surprised by Joy* and "Early Prose Joy," Lewis emphasizes that he saw the illustration and read the words *Siegfried and The Twilight of the Gods* next to it—a fact that has received little attention until now.

According to Roger Lancelyn Green and Walter Hooper, it was the Christmas edition of *The Bookman* (December 1911) that fell into Lewis's hands, which contained a supplement printed in color with several Rackham illustrations of the *Ring*.[5] However, this is not so. The *Christmas Double Number* of *The Bookman* (which is also the December issue) was accompanied by a 138-page *Christmas Supplement* in black and white, as well as a *Portfolio* with three color plates by Hugh Thomson (being illustrations for R. B. Sheridan's *The School for Scandal; see image 1*). Neither the 1911 Christmas edition nor the supplement contains any of Rackham's illustrations for *Siegfried and The Twilight of the Gods*;[6] the latter

---

[4] C. S. Lewis, "'Early Prose Joy': C. S. Lewis's Early Draft of an Autobiographical Manuscript" in *VII: An Anglo-American Literary Review*, 30 (2013), 16. This was published by Andrew Lazo. See Andrew Lazo, "'Early Prose Joy': A Brief Introduction," in *VII: An Anglo-American Literary Review*, 30 (2013), 5-12.

[5] Roger Lancelyn Green and Walter Hooper, *C. S. Lewis: A Biography* (New York: Harcourt Brace, 1994), 31. Alister McGrath's and Harry Lee Poe's biographies make a similar claim but do not cite their sources or add further evidence. While Lewis speaks of only one image, all three (Green and Hooper too) seem to assume that Lewis saw a supplement with several illustrations.

[6] The title page of the *Christmas Double Number* states that it has a cover plate by

does contain an advertisement for the volume on page 127, but it is not illustrated.[7]

While Lewis speaks of an *advertisement* for the Rackham volume, George Sayer in his 1988 biography *Jack*[8] claims that Lewis got hold of a magazine which contained a *review* of the Rackham volume and featured an illustration: a painting of Siegfried looking down on the sleeping Brünnhilde in the light of the rising sun whose breast plate he has removed so that her naked breasts are visible (see right, plate 13/30 of Rackham's illustrations). However, Sayer cites no source for this assertion;[9] on the contrary, he quotes the verses printed in Rackham's volume on the left-hand page (facing the illustration)[10] and adds that these verses were presumably not reproduced in the review. It therefore appears that Sayer never saw the review himself, which he claims was the trigger for Lewis's experience.

The actual source of Lewis's teenage encounter with Northernness appears to have eluded biographers thus far. After an exhaustive search, I have only been able to find one issue of a contemporary literary journal

---

Edmund Dulac and contains other (unspecified) full-page plates with pictures by Arthur Rackham, Charles Robinson, Claude A. Shepperson and Willy Pogány. However, such plates are not part of the *Portfolio*, nor of the Christmas edition, nor of the *Supplement*! I have not yet been able to solve this mystery.

[7] The U.S. magazine of the same name (*The Bookman*) in its 1911 Christmas issue ran a full-page reproduction of plate 1/30 (on page 383) but with the subtitle "SIEGFRIED BY ARTHUR RACKHAM."

[8] George Sayer, *Jack: A Life of C. S. Lewis* (Wheaton, Illinois: Crossway Books, 1994), 76.

[9] It is theoretically possible that Lewis told Sayer in a personal conversation that it was this painting he saw, but Sayer himself does not make this claim.

[10] "Mystical rapture / Pierces my heart; / Burning with terror; / I reel, my heart faints and fails" (Wagner, *Siegfried and Twilight of the Gods,* 86). These are Siegfried's words when, after removing the breastplate, he realises that the person in front of him is not a man but a woman. This four-liner is repeated on the left-hand page opposite the illustration (which is otherwise blank).

that contains the combination of said illustration and the words *Siegfried and The Twilight of the Gods*. In the popular U.S. magazine *The Literary Digest*, a reproduction of plate 29/30 from the Rackham volume appeared on 30 December 1911 with the caption *Siegfried and The Twilight of the Gods*. The picture shows Brünnhilde in the evening light jumping her horse Grane onto the funeral pyre where the dead Siegfried is being burned.

SIEGFRIED AND THE TWILIGHT OF THE GODS.
From a drawing by Arthur Rackham for this season's crop of Christmas books.

Are there reasons to suppose that it was this illustration which Lewis saw? I think so—because of the memory of Balder which both Rackham's illustration and the words printed next to it triggered in him. In his poem "Tegnér's Drapa",[11] Longfellow says of the dead Balder:

> They laid him in his ship,
> With horse and harness,
> As on a funeral pyre....
> They launched the burning ship!
> It floated far away
> Over the misty sea,
> Till like the sun it seemed,
> Sinking beneath the waves.
> Balder returned no more![12]

---

[11] Henry Wadsworth Longfellow, "Tegnér's Drapa," in *The Poetical Works of Henry Wadsworth Longfellow* (London: Fredrick Warne, 1868), 216-18. https://archive.org/details/poeticalworksofh00long_1/page/216/mode/2up?q=balder. Accessed 7 January 2023.

[12] Longfellow, "Tegnér's Drapa," 217-18, lines 37-9 and 43-8.

Here, too, a dead god is handed over to a funeral pyre and a horse appears. Longfellow also immerses his scene in the light of the setting sun, which may have contributed to Lewis's (mis)interpretation of the *Siegfried and The Twilight of the Gods* as evening.[13]

The similarity between the two scenes is unmistakable, and this could be the reason why Rackham's image evoked the memory of the dead Balder in Lewis, and he intuitively knew that Siegfried belonged to the same world as Balder. The images which arose in his mind apparently also resembled the imagery of Longfellow's poem.

And there is a second, somewhat less obvious, reason. In "Early Prose Joy," Lewis explains:

> I saw that twilight hanging pale and motionless over the Atlantic, slowly fading through the endless summer evening of the North: I saw those gods wheeling through it aloft on flying horses: I think (but of this I am uncertain) [that] even then, from some forgotten source, I supplied them with winged helmets.

Lewis's hesitation about the winged helmets suggests that he *was certain* about the flying horses—that they were part of the original vision and not a later back-projection. Longfellow, who, according to "Early Prose Joy", was Lewis's only source for Norse mythology up to that point, does not mention flying horses anywhere. So, the question arises as to how Lewis came up with the idea of having his gods fly on horses—unless the picture itself gave him cause to do so. Now Brünnhilde on Grane is the only illustration in the volume that shows a deity on a horse. This alone does not

---

[13] Balder is referred to in Longfellow as the god of the summer sun, so that his burial coincides with the sunset; Lewis's vision is marked by the fading of the summer evening of the north.

The Ride of the Valkyrs
J. C. Dollman
By Arrangement with the Artist

seen gods on flying horses. It is conceivable, however, that he had seen paintings of flying gods somewhere else, and that the illustration evoked the memory of these paintings in him. The *Edda*, which Lewis came to know only afterwards, features horses as mounts of the gods, and Wagner's Valkyries are also often depicted on flying horses. Rackham's illustration may have evoked the memory of such a painting Lewis had once seen, for example in H. A. Guerber's *Myths of the Norsemen*.[14] In the picture *The Ride of the Valkyries* by J. C. Dollman that is printed in this volume, the goddesses also wear winged helmets.[15]

We cannot be certain that *The Literary Digest* was available at Cher-

---

[14] H. A. Guerber, *Myths of the Norsemen from the Eddas and Sagas* (London: Harrap, 1909), 176. https://archive.org/details/mythsofthenorsem00gueruoft. Accessed 7 January 2023.

[15] When Lewis first visited his sick neighbour Arthur Greeves in April 1914, it was Guerber's *Myths of the Norsemen* that he saw on a table beside the bed (See Lewis, *Surprised by Joy*, 130 [end of Chapter 8 "Release"]). Unfortunately, it is not known when he first read this book. Rackham's first volume of *Ring* illustrations *The Rhinegold and The Valkyrie* also features the Valkyries riding flying horses, but Lewis didn't see this volume until later. Whether he had a glimpse of this volume before he received it as a natal gift from his father in the Christmas holidays of 1913/14 is not known. See letter of 24 November 1913 to Albert Lewis, in C. S. Lewis, *The Collected Letters of C. S. Lewis*, ed. by Walter Hooper, 3 vols. (San Francisco: HarperCollins, 2004-7), 1:40.

bourg House. *The Bookman* and *The Times Literary Supplement* are more likely suspects to be found in the school's library or common room. As we have seen though, the archives reveal that they contain no illustrations of *Siegfried and The Twilight of the Gods*. Thus, if Lewis really saw the image of Brünnhilde jumping with Grane onto the funeral pyre of the dead Siegfried, his reaction to both image and title would find an easy explanation. In the spirit of a cautious suggestion, it remains an open question whether Lewis actually saw this image in *The Literary Digest* or in some other unknown magazine. The combination of his description of a Rackham illustration titled with the exact phrase, *Siegfried and The Twilight of the Gods*, suggests, in my opinion, that we are on the right track. It would be a striking coincidence if another literary journal had published exactly the same combination of image and caption at about the same time.

So the hunt is on: if someone should find the combination of image and title mentioned by Lewis in a British magazine (whether with the same illustration or a different one), and/or should put forward an equally plausible or even more plausible idea of what Lewis might have seen in his schoolroom at Cherbourg House, I'd be delighted—I'm sure we all would be delighted—to hear about it!

Meanwhile, when we bring together the autobiography *Surprised by Joy* with the recently published evidence of "Early Prose Joy," the *Literary Digest* advertisement remains strikingly resonant of Lewis's profound teenage encounter with Northernness.

The Reading Life of Young Jack Lewis, 1914-1917

HARRY LEE POE

When young Jack Lewis had a disastrous experience at Malvern College, Albert Lewis sent his son to live with Albert's old headmaster who had retired to Great Bookham, Surrey. The elder Lewis hoped that the old man could prepare young Lewis for entry to Oxford and a profitable career. From the fall of 1914 until the winter of 1917, Lewis studied with W. T. Kirkpatrick and mastered the academic texts that Kirkpatrick assigned him to read. While these studies prepared Lewis to win a scholarship to Oxford, the pleasure reading which Lewis enjoyed in the evenings prepared him for a career as an English literature teacher and scholar while laying the tracks on which his conversion and calling as an apologist would emerge.[1]

When Lewis arrived in Great Bookham, he had the dream of becoming a great poet. After living with Kirkpatrick a short time, however, he resolved to become a philosopher. He did not exactly abandon the dream of poetry, but he developed divided loyalties. He planned to go up to Oxford where he intended to excel. First, he would undergo optional "Mods" (Classical Honour Moderations), the public Greek and Latin examinations, because

---

[1] For an in-depth discussion of the part played by Lewis's pleasure reading on his later life, see Harry Lee Poe, *Becoming C. S. Lewis* (Wheaton, IL: Crossway, 2019), 143-70, 182-85, 191-93, 195-96, 209-20. For a treatment of the literary influences on Lewis leading up to his conversion, see Joel D. Heck, *From Atheism to Christianity* (St. Louis: Concordia, 2017), 29-45. For a treatment of primarily religious books which influenced the mature Lewis, see James Stuart Bell and Anthony P. Dawson, *From the Library of C. S. Lewis* (New York: Doubleday, 2004).

as he explained to his father, "People might feel that they could never be quite sure of you unless they knew what you had done in Mods."[2] Then he would win a first in *Literae Humaniores*, known in Oxford as "Greats" (classical philosophy and history). Finally, he would be invited to be a fellow of one of the more prestigious colleges where he would teach philosophy. That was the plan. A war intervened, but by July 1922, he had completed the plan, except no college invited him to become a fellow. He had no alternate plan.

Preparation for a Career

Those who live an academic life have long been fond of extolling the value of learning for learning's sake and that a university does not prepare a student for a job but for a well-lived life. It is a lovely sentiment for the independently wealthy who never plan to work, but C. S. Lewis needed a job and he could not get one doing the only thing he was qualified to do. Therefore, he stayed on at Oxford for another year and took a second bachelor's degree in English literature in hopes that it would make him more attractive as a job applicant.

Lewis had a great intellect, but intellect alone is not enough to earn a degree from Oxford University in one year. Unlike an American university degree based on the number of hours a student has sat through lectures, an Oxford degree is based on what a student has learned. Students do not take a set number of courses filled with tests, quizzes, and exams. Instead, for an hour each week they meet with a tutor who guides their reading and for whom they prepare a paper of 3,000 to 5,000 words. The process is designed to prepare students to take one test in which they are expected to know everything on the subject. In the course of the tutorials, students are guided in their reading. Lewis was able to complete a degree in English literature in only one year because he had already done most of the reading as his pleasure reading at "Gastons," Kirkpatrick's house in Great Bookham.

Lewis liked routine, and at Gastons he fell into a regular pattern that divided his day between work with Kirkpatrick and free time to do as he

---

[2] C. S. Lewis, *The Collected Letters of C. S. Lewis*, ed. by Walter Hooper, 3 vols. (New York: HarperSanFrancisco, 2004-7), 1:438.

pleased with little supervision. His daily schedule involved:[3]

    8:00 Breakfast
    9:15 Greek lessons
    11:00 Break
    11:15 Latin lessons
    1:00 Lunch and free time
    5:00 Lessons
    7:00 Break
    7:30 Dinner and English literature

By 9:00, he was free to read what he liked. Decades later, Lewis still regarded this schedule as the ideal life—a schedule he had not had the freedom to follow, but the schedule he would like to have followed.[4]

When he went to Gastons, Lewis's favorite pleasure reading was Norse mythology, but his field of reading quickly expanded. Norse mythology led him to William Morris and his *The Well at the World's End*. Morris led him to Malory's *Le Morte D'Arthur*, which led him to Crétien de Troyes's *The High History of the Holy Graal*. Chrétien led him to Edmund Spenser's *The Faerie Queene*. (In 1936, he published a book about them called *The Allegory of Love*, and it established him as one of the new lions of English literary criticism. It all began with a little light reading.) He wrote to Arthur Greeves in January 1915 of his purchase of Malory's *Arthur*, which he had ordered on 17 November 1914: "I am more pleased at having bought it every day, as it has opened up a new world to me."[5] The new world was in the plot.

Preparation for Conversion to Christianity

What all these stories have in common is their plot. It is the "journey story." The hero ventures forth on a great quest for which he abandons everything. He must go to the ends of the world in search of the great

---

[3] Lewis, *Collected Letters*, 1:78.
[4] C. S. Lewis, *Surprised by Joy* (London: Geoffrey Bless, 1955), 135-6. In this ideal life, he would have taken tea alone no later than 4:15 during which he would be free to read "formless books which can be opened anywhere," like Boswell's Life of Johnson.
[5] Lewis, *Collected Letters*, 1:103.

thing beyond worth, but along the way he must fight many battles often to rescue a damsel in distress. Once he reaches the prize, he returns home as a person who has been changed in the course of the quest. Lewis loved this plot all his life. He wrote scholarly books about it. His science fiction novels and Narnia tales relate this plot, and when he first came to narrate his conversion to Christianity, he used this plot to tell *The Pilgrim's Regress*. He did not know it when he first read it, but he would discover that this plot is the allegory of the Christian story. Encountering the plot reinforced for Lewis his occasional experience of that longing for something that he called Joy, which nothing seemed to satisfy.

His reading of the other great stories of the English language tradition also had a spiritual effect on him. While W. T. Kirkpatrick filled his head with a materialist interpretation of reality during the day, the fiction he read filled his head with a deep longing for a reality beyond this world. In a materialist world, there are no values, just brute matter. Nothing is right or wrong, good or bad, beautiful or ugly. Things just are.[6] Yet, Lewis fell in love with the values expressed by the Brontë sisters, Jane Austen, and all the rest. His pleasure reading brought him to a state of cognitive dissonance between the values he found in the great literature of the western tradition and the materialist philosophy which Kirkpatrick had fed him. Decades later, long after his conversion, he explained it this way: "Nearly all that I loved I believed to be imaginary; nearly all that I believed to be real I thought grim and meaningless."[7]

Preparation for Apologetics

From the values he found in the journey story, Lewis's pleasure reading eventually compelled him to account for morality and the universal sense of right and wrong. Where do they come from? Any explanation would have to satisfy the logical training he had received from Kirkpatrick. The question became a chief topic of conversation for Lewis in the 1920s, as well as the subject of papers he wrote and his first set of lectures in the year he taught philosophy for University College before gaining a fellowship in literature at Magdalen. The titles of the lectures were "The Good, its

---

[6] Lewis, *Surprised by Joy*, 163.
[7] Lewis, *Surprised by Joy*, 161.

position among the values" and "Moral Good, its position among the values."[8]

In his desperation as evidenced throughout the diary he kept between 1922 and 1927, Lewis sought to disprove what he called the "Promethean attitude."[9] In Greek mythology, the titan Prometheus took fire, the exclusive property of the gods, and gave it to humans. The Promethean attitude was the view that moral consciousness had come from outside the material world, just as Prometheus had brought fire to humans from the gods. Lewis did not see how that could be possible, however, since he believed that nothing existed beyond the physical world. Instead of disproving this view, Lewis ended up adopting the Promethean attitude and proving to himself that "right and wrong [are] a clue to the meaning of the universe" and that values come as a gift from God.[10] It all had begun with his pleasure reading at Gastons. As he would glibly remark about his youthful reading habits, "A young man who wishes to remain a sound Atheist cannot be too careful of his reading."[11]

His reluctant belief in the reality of values became the starting point of Lewis's conversion and the foundation for his later apologetics. It is the opening salvo of his radio broadcasts which became *Mere Christianity*. It is also the foundational issue on which he developed *The Abolition of Man*. And it all began with a little light reading.

What Young Lewis Read

What follows is a list of what young Lewis read for his lessons with W. T. Kirkpatrick (over 50 works) and what he read for pleasure (over 150 works). He probably read more than this, but this is all that can be documented. We know that he read many of these books two times or more while at Gastons, because his letters to Arthur Greeves every week were full of discussions of what he was reading at the time. The choice of books which Kirkpatrick put before Lewis foreshadows a point Lewis would make in *The Abolition of Man* about "a boy who thinks he is 'doing'

---

[8] C. S. Lewis, *All My Road Before Me*, ed. by Walter Hooper (New York: Harcourt Brace Jovanovich, 1991), 348.
[9] Lewis, *All My Road Before Me*, 281.
[10] C. S. Lewis, *Mere Christianity* (New York: Macmillan, 1952), 1.
[11] Lewis, *Surprised by Joy*, 181.

his 'English prep' and has no notion that ethics, theology, and politics are all at stake."[12] The reading Lewis did at Gastons enriched his mind, but it also ignited his heart and fanned the spark he called Joy.[13]

W. T. Kirkpatrick's Assigned Reading List[14]

Greek and Latin
Aeschylus 158
    The Agamemnon (Lewis Family Papers, 5:12)[15]
Apollonius 278
    Argonautica (209, 221) [cf. William Morris translation]
Apuleius
    "Cupid and Psyche in *The Golden Ass* (268)
Catullus (288)
Cicero (137)
Demosthenes (137)
    De Corona (Lewis Family Papers, 5:12)
Euripides (158)
    Helena (107)
Gesta Romanorum (268)
Herodotus
    Histories (284)
Horace 200
    Epistles (152)
Homer (167)
    The Iliad (71, 128)
    The Odyssey (102, 152)
Lucan (199)
Lucretius (trans. Bacon) (238)
    Tantum religio (*Surprised by Joy*, 162)

---

[12] C. S. Lewis, *The Abolition of Man* (New York: Macmillan, 1947), 3.

[13] For a full discussion of the influence of Lewis's experience at Gastons between 1914 and 1917 on his conversion experience the following decade in Oxford, see Harry Lee Poe, *Becoming C. S. Lewis* (Wheaton, IL: Crossway, 2019) and Harry Lee Poe, *The Making of C. S. Lewis* (Wheaton, IL: Crossway, 2021).

[14] All numbers following authors and/or titles in the list refer to page numbers in volume one of Hooper's *The Collected Letters of C. S. Lewis*, except where indicated.

[15] Letter of 17 August 1915, from W. T. Kirkpatrick to C. S. Lewis ("Clive"), in Warren Hamilton Lewis, ed., MS *Memoirs of the Lewis Family,1850-1930*, Wade-A-110, 1933-5, Marion E. Wade Center Collection, Wheaton College, Wheaton, IL, 5:12. These papers edited by Major Lewis are often referred to colloquially as the *Lewis Family Papers*.

Ovid (154)
Plato
    The Phaedo (Lewis Family Papers, 5:12)
Pindar (193, 199)
Tacitus
    Annals (234, 284), (Lewis Family Papers, 5:12)
    Germania (284)
    Histories (284)
    The Life of Agricola (102, 284)
Virgil
    Aeneid (112, 128, 157, 177)

Secondary:
Lang, Andrew
    History of English Literature (157)
    The Odyssey of Homer (trans. S. A. Butcher and Andrew Lang), (238)
Murray, Gilbert
    A History of Ancient Greek Literature (158)

French
Chénier, André
    Poésies (219)
Froissart
    Froissart's Chronicles (287)
Maeterlinck, Maurice
    La Mort (270, 274)
    Oiseau Bleu (239)
Nadier, Charles
    Contes Fantastique (273)
Paris, Gaston
    Litérature Française du Moyen Age (269, 278, 282)
Rousseau, Jean-Jacques
    Les Confessions (282, 285)
Voltaire
    Contes (274)

German
Chamisso
    The Amazing Adventure of Peter Schlemiel (276, 286, 289)
Fouqué, Friedrich
    Sintram and his Companions (289)
    Undine (289)

English
Bacon, Francis
  Essays or Counsels, Civil and Moral (121)
Bennett, Arnold
  How to Form Literary Taste (240, 246)
Benson, A. C.
  Upton Letters (160)
Boas, F. S. 237, 243
  Shakespeare and His Predecessors (238)
Boswell, James (234, 241)
  The Life of Samuel Johnson (228)
Bridges, Robert
  The Spirit of Man (166)
Burrell, Arthur
  British Ballads: English Literature for Schools (170, 173)
Clodd, Edward
  Memoirs (251)
Collins, William
  The Poetical Works of Gray and Collins (269)
Green, John Richard
  Short History of the English People (245)
Lang, Andrew (284)
  History of English Literature (157)
  The Odyssey of Homer (trans. S. A. Butcher and Andrew Lang), (238)
Mackail, John William
  Springs of Helicon: A Study in the Progress of English Poetry from Chaucer to Milton (157)
Pater, Walter
  Renaissance (219)
Ruskin, John (247)
  A Joy Forever (165)
Schopenhauer, Arthur
  The World as Will and Idea (151)
Swinburne, Algernon Charles (174, 238)
  A Study of Shakespeare (107)

Jack's Pleasure Reading at Gastons[16]

Ainsworth, William Harrison (92)
Anderson, Hans Christian
  The Mermaid and Other Fairy Tales (119)

---

[16] All numbers following authors and/or titles in this list refer to page numbers in volume one of *The Collected Letters of C. S. Lewis*, except where noted.

Arnold, Matthew
    "Balder Dead" (220)
Austey, F.
    The Talking Horse and Other Tales (272)
Austen, Jane (174, 235, 239, 245, 256, 287)
    Emma (182, 197)
    Mansfield Park (129, 182, 281)
    Northanger Abbey (181, 257)
    Persuasion (181, 186)
    Pride and Prejudice (260)
    Sense and Sensibility (70, 223)
Bail, Francis William
    The Descent of the Sun (274)
    The Heifer of the Dawn (274, 278)
Beowulf (244)
Blackwood, Algernon
    The Complete John Silence Stories (201, 214, 215, 219, 270)
    The Education of Uncle Paul (161)
    Jimbo: A Fantasy (222, 224, 225)
Brontë, Anne
    The Tenant of Wildfell Hall (284, 290)
Brontë, Charlotte (201, 281)
    Jane Eyre (117, 161, 202)
    The Professor (245)
    Shirley (117, 174, 180, 189, 211)
    Villette (102, 117)
Brontë, Emily
    Wuthering Heights (202, 258)
Brontës (170, 180, 236, 260, 290)
Bunyan, John
    The Pilgrim's Progress (247, 254)
Burney, Frances
    Evelina (233)
Burns, Robert
    "To a Mouse" (177)
Burrow, George
    Lavengro (236)
Byron, George Gordon, Lord
    The Destruction of Sennacherib (154)
Carroll, Lewis
    Alice in Wonderland (272)
Chaucer 250
    Canterbury Tales (183, 185, 187, 192)
    Troilus and Criseyde (156, 157, 239)

Chénier (*Surprised by Joy*, 140)
Clufton-Brock, Arthur
    William Morris: His Worth and Influence (117, 118)
Crawford, Francis Marion
    Arethusa (272, 274)
Chrétien de Troyes
    The High History of the Holy Graal (249, 254)
Dante (275)
De Quincey, Thomas (199, 285)
    Confessions of an English Opium Eater (113, 181, 182, 187, 192, 199)
Dickens, Charles
    David Copperfield (154)
Dumas, Alexander (293)
Edda (249)
Gaskell, Elizabeth Cleghorn
    Cranford (235, 239)
    The Life of Charlotte Brontë (285, 289, 290, 291)
Goldsmith, Oliver (174)
    The Vicar of Wakefield (69)
Goethe (97)
Gray, Thomas
    The Poetical Works of Gray and Collins (269)
Haggard, H. Rider
    Pearl Maiden (165)
Hankey, Donald
    A Student in Arms (242)
Hardy, Thomas
    Under the Greenwood Tree (211)
Hart, Bret (154)
Hawthorne, Nathaniel
    House of the Seven Gables (256, 258, 261)
Henty, George (105)
Herrick, Robert (*Surprised by Joy*, 140)
Hewlett, Maurice
    The Lore of Proserpine (162, 168)
Hugo, Victor
    Hans d'Islande (290, 293)
    Les Miserables (270)
Ibsen, Henrik (78)
James, Henry (274)
Keats, John (98, 288, 290)
    "Endymion" (220)
    "The Eve of St. Agnes" (220)

Kalevala (222, 226, 228, 232, 235)
Kingsley, Charles
    Westward Ho! (184)
Kipling, Rudyard (233, 236, 237)
    The Jungle Book (106)
    Kim (106)
    Puck (106)
    Rewards and Fairies (236)
    The Seven Seas (106)
Lamb, Charles
    The Last Essays of Elia (242)
    "The Superannuated Man" (226)
    A Tale of Rosamund Gray and Old Blind Margaret (278)
Landor, Walter Savage
    Pericles and Aspasia (110)
Laxdaela Saga [Icelandic saga of Gudrun] (128, 129)
Layamon
    Brut (162)
Lockhart, John Gibson
    The Life of Scott (240)
Longfellow, Henry Wadsworth
    "The Village Blacksmith" (154)
    "The Wreck of the Hesperus" (154)
Macauley, Thomas (238, 247, 274, 277, 281)
Macdonald, George (236, 252)
    At the Back of the North Wind (175, 180)
    Phantastes (169, 173, 175, 189, 206, 258, 281, 293)
    Sir Gibbie (175)
    "The Golden Key" in *Works of Fancy and Imagination* (254, 257)
Malory (235, 244, 245, 249, 274, 278)
    Morte D'Arthur (94, 103, 128, 192, 196, 207, 227, 229, 232, 239)
Mandeville, Sir John (*Surprised by Joy*, 140)
    The Travels of Sir John Mandeville [ed. A. W. Pollard] (214)
Mayne, Colburn[?] (173)
Merriman, Henry Seton
    The Grey Lady (103)
    With Edged Tools (103)
Milton, John (182, 183, 215, 232)
    Paradise Lost (94, 199, 214, 215, 220, 269, 278, 290)
    Paradise Regained and Minor Poems (225, 227, 232)
Mitford, Mary Russell
    Our Village (239)

Morris, William (218, 249, 274, 278, 281, 282, 287, 288, 290)
    Earthly Paradise (220)
    Grettir Saga: The Story of Grettir the Strong (165)
    The Life and Death of Jason (201, 207, 209, 221, 269, 282, 293)
    Lyric Poems (92)
    The Roots of the Mountains (119, 122, 128)
    Rapunzel (227)
    Sigurd the Volsung (92)
    Völsunga Saga: The Story of the Volsungs and Niblungs, with Certain Songs from the Elder Edda (trans. By Eirikir Magnusson and William Morris) (165, 168)
    The Well at the World's End (92, 94, 122, 128, 153, 169, 245, 270)
Osborne, Dorothy
    Letters of Dorothy Osborne to Sir William Temple (ed. by E. A. Perry) (230, 239, 241, 250, 254, 256)
Peacock, Thomas Love
    Headlong Hall (150)
Poe, Edgar Allan, (290)
    "The Raven" (199)
Ronsard, Pierre de (*Surprised by Joy*, 140)
Rossetti, Dante Gabriel (220)
Sand, George
    Tales of a Grandmother (274)
Scott, Sir Walter 225, 245, 293
    The Antiquary (232, 235, 236, 249, 254, 257)
    The Fair Maid of Perth (240)
    Guy Mannering (240, 257, 260)
    Ivanhoe (211, 240)
    Quentin Durward (240)
    Rob Roy (180, 183, 184, 185, 186, 190, 293)
    Tales of a Grandfather (259)
Shakespeare, William
    As You Like It (69)
    A Midsummer Night's Dream (246)
    Othello (132)
    Sonnets (246)
    The Tempest (246)
    Twelfth Night (214, 220)
    The Winter's Tale (246)
Shaw, George Bernard (242)
    Love Among the Artists (190)
Shelley, Mary
    Frankenstein (181, 183, 187, 189)

Shelley, Percy Bysshe (98)
    Adonis (110)
    "Ode to the West Wind" (290)
    "Prometheus Unbound" (232)
    "To – : One Word is too often Profaned" (198)
Sidney, Sir Philip
    Arcadia (196, 199, 201, 205, 207, 211, 214)
Sir Gawain and the Green Knight (180, 192)
Song of Roland (207, 212)
Southey, Robert (199)
Spenser, Edmund (240, 246)
    The Fairie Queene (106, 151, 152, 157, 160, 161, 165, 169, 170, 175, 196, 223, 225)
Stephens, James 236
    The Crock of Gold (196, 281, 293)
Sterne, Laurence
    The Life and Opinions of Tristram Shandy (241)
Swinburne, Algernon Charles (174, 238)
    Atalanta in Calydon (151)
    Erechtheas (151)
    Poems and Ballads (112)
Tennyson, Alfred, Lord
    "Break, Break, Break" (172)
Thisted, Valdemar Adolph
    Letters from Hell (215, 219, 225, 232, 236, 256)
Thackeray, William Makepeace
    Henry Esmond (104)
    History of Pendennis (210, 213, 217, 220)
    The Newcomes (223, 225)
    Vanity Fair (281)
Tristan and Iseult (trans. Joseph Bédier, French edition), (183, 195, 196, 207)
Tristan and Iseult (Matthew Arnold), (220)
Trollope, Anthony (174)
Troly-Curtin, Marthe
    Phrynette and London (222)
Twain, Mark (154)
Vachell, Horace Annesley
    The Paladin (228)
Walton (*Surprised by Joy*, 140)
Ward, Mary Augusta
    Lady Connie (230, 234, 251)
Wells, H. G.
    The Country of the Blind, and Other Stories (70-71, 246)

Wordsworth, William 154
    The Prelude (*Surprised by Joy*, 158)
Yeats, William Butler
    Plays for an Irish Theatre (90)

Three University College Tutors: Arthur Blackburne Poynton, E. F. Carritt, and George Hope Stevenson

JOEL D. HECK

When C. S. Lewis returned from serving in France during World War I, anxious to begin his university studies, one of the first people he met at Oxford University was his tutor in the Classics (Greek and Latin language and literature), Arthur Blackburne Poynton. Poynton's combination of scholarship, warmth, and irreligion undoubtedly influenced Lewis in significant ways. Poynton was one of the three most important tutors that instructed him during his undergraduate years, all of them amiable and scholarly. The second was the philosopher E. F. Carritt, and the third was George Hope Stevenson.[1] At this time when Lewis was trying to be a consistent materialist, and the positions of both Poynton and Carritt on religion seemed to undergird this commitment to materialism.

Lewis and Poynton, Lewis and Carritt, Lewis and Stevenson—student and tutors, a student of the Classics, philosophy, and history taught by professional scholars—were people who also formed a bond of friendship. Though they became more distant when Lewis became a Christian, no doubt to the disappointment of both Poynton and Carritt, the original respect that Lewis had for his tutors never waned, even when Carritt weighed in on a minor controversy Lewis had with S. L. Bethel and George

---

[1] Lewis took another year to earn a First in English language and literature, where his tutors were F. P. Wilson and George Gordon.

Every. If W. T. Kirkpatrick taught Lewis how to think, Poynton, Carritt, and Stevenson fine-tuned that thinking and enabled Lewis to rise to even greater heights that would serve him well as a young teacher of philosophy, aided by his knowledge of the Classics, a lover of history, and eventually the author of such books as *The Abolition of Man* and *Miracles*.

Classics Tutor Arthur Blackburne Poynton

Poynton, 1905
(Balliol College Historic Collections, PHOT23.01)

Arthur Blackburne Poynton was born on 28 June 1867 in southwestern England at Kelston, Somerset, just four miles north of Bath, the son of the Rev. Francis John Poynton and Frances Mary Billinge. He attended Marlborough College and entered Balliol College, Oxford, in 1885.[2] Poynton was considered "one of the most distinguished undergraduate scholars of his generation."[3] He earned a First in Honor Moderations, a Craven Scholarship in 1887, a First in *Literae Humaniores* in 1889, and in 1890 he was elected a Fellow of Hertford College.[4]

In 1896, Poynton married Mary Sargent, the oldest daughter of Hertford College Fellow John Young Sargent. Arthur and Mary had two sons, the classical scholar John Blackburne Poynton, who followed in his father's footsteps, and the civil servant Sir Arthur Hilton Poynton, who served as the Permanent Under-Secretary of State for the Colonies, and they also had three daughters, Winifred, Helen, and Anna.

One author describes Poynton as a man of "medium height, with a fresh complexion and very direct gray eyes. His hair was dark and, despite all his hard work and the passage of time, it was only lightly touched with grey. I may say that he was sometimes a little absent-minded, as a man with

---

[2] "Obituary," in *The Times*, 10 October 1944, 6. Most of the biographical sketch, except where noted, is derived from Wikipedia.

[3] Walter Hooper, Biographical Appendix, "Poynton, Arthur Blackburne," in C. S. Lewis, *All My Road Before Me: The Diary of C. S. Lewis, 1922-1927*, ed. by Walter Hooper (New York: Harcourt, Brace, Jovanovich, 1991), 468.

[4] Hooper, "Poynton, Arthur Blackburne," 468. See also "Obituary," in *The Times*, 10 October 1944, 6. Honour Moderations was the study of Greek and Latin language and literature, while *Literae Humaniores* was a course of study in ancient history and philosophy.

all his preoccupations might well be."[5]

Poynton was a Fellow of Hertford College, Oxford, until 1894 when he was elected a Fellow and Tutor at University College, where he spent the rest of his career. His teaching field was Greek and Latin language and literature, that is, the Classics, and he was one of two Classics Fellows at University College (usually called Univ. in Oxford), the other being Arthur Farquharson.[6] Since in Oxford, "Classics dominated university examinations from their foundation,"[7] Poynton taught at the pinnacle of an Oxonian education. Poynton was considered "not merely as one of the most brilliant of classical teachers, but one of the most able and accurate of scholars." And one of the most hard-working. He has been described by one who knew him as "a most popular lecturer."[8]

Poynton's expertise was in Greek oratory,[9] especially rhetoric, Isocrates,[10] and Cicero.[11] He lectured on Cicero's speeches, Plato's *Republic*, Aristotle's *Poetics*, and Tacitus's *Annals*, and occasionally on Lucretius, but would occasionally lecture on Attic orators, Aristotle's *Rhetoric*, or the Greek writers.[12] E. R. Dodds writes, "He saw the task of scholarship not as the reinterpretation of ancient masterpieces or the rediscovery of ancient modes of thought, but simply as the transmission of the most exact possible knowledge of two ancient languages. This implies that Poynton took a philological, rather than critical/analytic, approach. Lewis was more analytic in his approach and put value on rediscovering ancient modes of thought. Poynton was an expert teacher, and he treated tutorial teaching as a form of intercollegiate competition into which he entered with zest."[13] His nickname was "The Poynt."

---

[5] Fred Bickerton, *Fred of Oxford* (London: Evans Brothers, 1953), 137.

[6] Farquharson helped produce a major revision of an important Greek lexicon, the *Liddell and Scott's Greek-English Lexicon*.

[7] Christopher Stray, "Curriculum and Style in the Collegiate University: Classics in Nineteenth Century-Oxbridge," in Christopher Stray, *Classics in Britain: Scholarship, Education, and Publishing 1800-2000* (Oxford: Oxford University Press, 2018), 42.

[8] Bickerton, *Fred of Oxford*, 137.

[9] Hooper, "Poynton, Arthur Blackburne," 468.

[10] A Greek orator and rhetorician who lived in Athens from 436 to 338 B.C.

[11] https://thereaderwiki.com/en/Arthur_Blackburne_Poynton.

[12] "Obituary," in *The Times*, 10 October 1944, 6.

[13] E. R. Dodds, *Missing Persons: An Autobiography* (Oxford: Clarendon Press, 1977), 26-7.

Poynton's familiarity with Lucretius would have resonated with Lewis.[14] The death of Lewis's mother in 1908 had convinced him that the world was cruel and meaningless, and Lewis found the words of Lucretius to reflect what he had felt for nearly a decade when he came to study in Oxford with Poynton. Lucretius had written,

> Had God designed the world, it would not be
> A world so frail and faulty as we see.[15]

The prayers that he was taught to say did not result in his mother's return to health, so he began to see the world as frail and faulty.[16]

At Univ., Poynton tutored C. S. Lewis from 13 January 1919, until Lewis began exams for Honour Moderations on 4 March 1920. During this period Lewis had adopted the "new look," excluding the supernatural, romanticism, pessimism, and self-pity,[17] and March was the month in which his irreverent cycle of poems, *Spirits in Bondage*, was published. The new look included hearing Cyril Bailey's "very amusing"[18] lecture on Lucretius in that first month. That same month, Warren Lewis wrote to his father, stating that it would have been better if *Spirits in Bondage* had never been published.[19]

E. F. Carritt's brief remarks about Poynton in his autobiography recall some of his strengths. "Both as Bursar and Master Poynton was the ideal

---

[14] Lewis wrote an undated essay on Lucretius, which appears in Adam Barkman, *C. S. Lewis and Philosophy as a Way of Life: A Comprehensive Historical Examination of His Philosophical Thoughts* (Cheshire, CT: Zossima Press, 2009), 533-4, and in C. S. Lewis, *Image and Imagination: Essays and Reviews*, ed. by Walter Hooper (Cambridge: Cambridge University Press, 2013), 194-7.

[15] C. S. Lewis, *Surprised by Joy: The Shape of My Early Life*. (San Diego: Harcourt Brace Jovanovich, 1955), 65. The Lucretius quote is from *De Rerum Natura*, Book 5, 198-99. According to *Surprised by Joy*, 144, he discovered this quotation at least as early as his time with Kirkpatrick (1914-7).

[16] Lewis, *Surprised by Joy*, 20, 21, 65.

[17] Lewis, *Surprised by Joy*, 201.

[18] C. S. Lewis, *They Stand Together: The Letters of C. S. Lewis to Arthur Greeves, 1914-1963*, ed. by Walter Hooper (New York: Macmillan, 1979), 242.

[19] Warren Lewis, MS *The Lewis Papers, Letters and Papers: Memoirs of the Lewis Family, 1850-1930*, vol. 6, 1933, Marion E. Wade Center, Wheaton, IL, 84. Cited in Don W. King, "Spirits in Bondage: A Cycle of Lyrics [Clive Hamilton, pseud.]," in *The C. S. Lewis Readers' Encyclopedia* (Grand Rapids: Zondervan, 1998), 385.

College patriot, he would devote all the energies of an acute mind to the intricacies of every financial or legal question, and it was his briefing of counsel that won for us our claim, as against the City, that, on the strength of ancient agreements and usage, Logic Lane was our property. He was a shy but friendly man, greatly valued as Classical Tutor by all serious pupils."[20]

Poynton served as Bursar (i.e., Business Manager) of Univ. from 1900 to 1935, as overseer of the Fellows' Garden (where, as Fellow Edmund Bowen observed, Poynton grew poisonous plants[21]), and as its Master from 1935 to 1937. His two years as Master were marked by two significant remodeling projects. Poynton's election as Master "was clearly a consolation prize, not least as he would have to retire after only two years."[22]

Poynton retired from Oxford in 1937 and was made an honorary fellow of his college. Although he did not publish much, he wrote *Cicero Pro Milone* (1892),[23] *Flosculi Latini* (Oxford: Clarendon Press, 1922[24]), *Isocrates* (London: Oxford University Press), *Flosculi Graeci* (Oxford: Clarendon Press, 1920), and *Gregory of Nazianzus and the Greek Rhetoricians* (Oxford: Academic Copying Office, 1934).

He was Public Orator at the University of Oxford for seven years, from 1925 to 1932, once delivering a lecture in Greek,[25] covering the speaking style of Isocrates.[26] He delivered the oration for Albert Einstein at Einstein's honorary degree ceremony in the Sheldonian Theatre on 23 May 1931. On 8 October 1944, at the age of 76, while crossing High Street in front of Univ., Poynton was killed by an automobile. His wife Mary outlived him by nine years.

---

[20] E. F. Carritt, *Fifty Years a Don* [Self-published] (1959), 59.

[21] Robin Darwall-Smith, *A History of University College Oxford* (Oxford: Oxford University Press, 2008), 416.

[22] Darwall-Smith, *A History of University College*, 452.

[23] Hooper, "Poynton, Arthur Blackburne," 468. The Latin means "Cicero for Milo," i.e., Cicero's speech on behalf of his friend Titus Annius Milo.

[24] https://openlibrary.org/. Search "Flosculi Latini." Accessed 2 January 2023. Literally, "Latin Flowers."

[25] That lecture took place in November 1927. See also "Obituary" in *The Times*, 10 October 1944, 6.

[26] Hooper, "Poynton, Arthur Blackburne," 468.

Lewis and Poynton

Lewis rated Poynton highly as a tutor. Shortly after his return to the university following World War II, Lewis wrote to his father about post-war university life, calling Poynton "quite an exceptionally good tutor" and "an excellent if somewhat unjust raconteur."[27] He repeats that rating and his growing appreciation of Poynton a month later, and again nearly three months after that.[28] Clearly, Poynton was effective.

E. R. Dodds writes about special training in the Classics which Poynton was known for:

> Besides the weekly compositions, further special training for selected colts in the form of 'Poynton's Friday evenings,' when three or four of us sat round the fire in his rooms, each with a glass of port to sustain him for the daunting task of translating Pindar viva voce without previous preparation.[29]

Lewis was undoubtedly one of Poynton's "selected colts" who engaged in some of this special training. Lewis had read Pindar as early as 1916 before coming up to Oxford University, and he later wrote the poem "Arrangement of Pindar," which was published by *Mandrake*.[30]

This relationship came during Lewis's atheistic phase of life, and he probably got no pushback from Poynton over his religious beliefs. Poynton, the son of a clergyman, seems not to have maintained his father's faith, given some of his opinions. He once remarked about the College Chaplain Rev. A. J. Carlyle, "Carlyle reads as much of the service as he can remember."[31] Although he was an atheist at this time, Lewis thought Poynton's comment only half-justified.[32] On another occasion, while in the midst of writing

---

[27] Letter of 4 February 1919, in C. S. Lewis, *The Collected Letters of C. S. Lewis*, ed. by Walter Hooper, 3 vols. (San Francisco: HarperCollins, 2004-7), 1:429-30.

[28] Letter of 5 March 1919, in Lewis, *Collected Letters*, 1:444. Lewis made a similar comment that May. See letter of 25 May 1919, in Lewis, *Collected Letters*, 1: 450.

[29] Dodds, *Missing Persons*, 27.

[30] Later titled "Pindar Sang." Jocelyn Gibb, ed. *Light on C. S. Lewis* (New York: Harcourt, Brace and World, 1965), 140. C. S. Lewis, *Poems* (New York; Harcourt Brace, 1964), 15-17; C. S. Lewis, *The Collected Poems of C. S. Lewis: A Critical Edition*, ed. by Don W. King (Kent, Ohio: Kent State University Press, 2015), 363-5.

[31] Letter of 28 February 1919, in Lewis, *Collected Letters*, 1:438.

[32] Lewis, *Collected Letters*, 1:438.

exams for Greats (elsewhere called *Literae Humaniores*, i.e., ancient history and philosophy), Lewis wrote in his diary that Poynton "had a vague belief in a future life,"[33] a comment whose accuracy we can probably trust.

Tutor and Bursar

Poynton and Lewis first met because of their tutorial relationship. Soon thereafter, Lewis decided to take the advice of Poynton, i.e., to take Honor Moderations rather than go directly to Greats.[34] Honor Moderations included the study of the Classics, Poynton's field. The advice was sound since it would help Lewis get a fellowship in the future.

Several years later, as the date for exams in Greats approached, Poynton gave Lewis a Latin prose piece to work on as a trial run.[35] A couple of months later, as Lewis continued preparing for exams, Poynton advised Ovid's *Metamorphoses* for "Unseens."[36] Poynton wanted Lewis to succeed.

Poynton had a personality full of life, intelligence, and humor, so engaging that the younger Lewis upon occasion told his older brother Warren some good stories he had heard from Poynton.[37] Early in his time at Univ., Lewis had tea with Mr. and Mrs. Poynton, their daughter, two female undergraduates, and another male undergraduate. He describes Poynton as "quite amusing," calling him "a very humorous old man who says the funniest things in a monotonous, melancholy voice,"[38] but, unfortunately, not specifically identifying any of those "funniest things." Because Poynton also served as the bursar of Univ. during the Lewis years, Lewis spoke to him about financial matters whenever necessary. On the day he received his B.A. degree, Lewis went to College after breakfast to see Poynton about

---

[33] Entry of 12 June 1922, in Lewis, *All My Road Before Me*, 48.

[34] The advice of Poynton is recorded in a letter dated 27 January 1919, in Lewis, *Collected Letters*, 1:428. Lewis had returned to Oxford precisely two weeks earlier on 13 January.

[35] Entry of 15 May 1922, in Lewis, *All My Road Before Me*, 35.

[36] That is, the translation of a passage the student has not previously seen. Entry of 10 July 1922, in Lewis, *All My Road Before Me*, 67.

[37] Warren Lewis's unpublished diary for this date: 20 August 1922. None of the actual stories appear in Warren's diary. Warren H. Lewis, MS *Warren H. Lewis Diary Collection*, vol. 6, WHL 1-49, 14 August 1922–8 December 1922, Marion E. Wade Center, Wheaton College, Wheaton, IL

[38] Entry of 2 February 1919, in Lewis, *All My Road Before Me*, 432.

money matters. He learned that he had a balance in his favor.[39] Later that year, Poynton suggested that Lewis's scholarship had likely been extended.[40]

Finding Employment

Oxford tutors often helped their students find employment during and after the completion of their education. Poynton was no exception, trying to help Lewis get an Oxford fellowship or at least some private students whom he could tutor and thereby earn some additional income. He offered to write a testimonial (recommendation) for Lewis if one was needed, especially in the time after Lewis earned his degree, and he advised him on a potential job at Reading University.[41]

Lewis once met Poynton in the Parks Road, where they talked about the vacancy at Univ. and some tutoring work for Lewis. This is remarkable, given the fact that Lewis had not studied under Poynton in more than three years. Poynton gave Lewis some hope that the Univ. position might belong to Lewis, and he promised to try to get him some tutoring among the women.[42] That fall during Michaelmas Term, Lewis went into town to visit Poynton. Poynton was once again trying to get Lewis some pupils. "After tea, wh. we had over the drawing room fire, I went into town again and visited Poynton in the Bursary.... He ... told me he was writing to two women to see if they cd. get me any pupils.... He said he was not without hopes for me and if they decided to elect a member of their own body, they would prefer no one to me.... He said I had many friends in college. Overall, his remarks were fairly encouraging."[43] But nothing came of it, at least for the moment.

Wining and Dining

As Poynton became more of a friend and eventually a colleague, this growing relationship demonstrated itself on various social occasions. Lewis had had a goal of attaining an Oxford Fellowship almost from the

---

[39] Letter of 5 August 1922, in Lewis, *They Stand Together*, 81.
[40] Entry 6 of 12 October 1922, in Lewis, *All My Road Before Me*, 117.
[41] Entry of 17 June 1922, in Lewis, *All My Road Before Me*, 52.
[42] Entry of 21 July 1923, in Lewis, *All My Road Before Me*, 259.
[43] Entry of 12 October 1923, in Lewis, *All My Road Before Me*, 271-2.

first day they met in January 1919. The first occasion for sharing wine came in June 1924 when Lewis was preparing to take on Carritt's tutorial duties in philosophy for the next year. Lewis was present because of Carritt, but Poynton was also present. After dinner, Poynton stood and handed out the wine to those who had come together in the Common Room. Lewis writes, "Poynton was in great form."[44] Poynton stated, "I am for the outward passage. We are thirteen and I got up first. It was just how it happened with poor Emmet. The only thing to do is to drink as much port as possible." After that Poynton provided them with an imitation of his idea of a Greek chorus, which was one of his specialties.[45]

Over the next year, Lewis dined with colleagues, as was his privilege. In spite of the cost, Lewis relished Poynton's companionship (and his cleverness), and that of the other dons, sometimes even after making a special trip into College for that purpose. Lewis once wrote, "Poynton and Farquharson both in and very amusing."[46] Apparently Lewis dined at Univ. on several occasions, and his frequent notes provide an indication of the high regard with which he held such dining.

One of the last recorded dinners at Univ. took place in 1928. Lewis wrote, "Poynton, the Fark, Carritt and Stevenson, as luck would have it, were all in that evening and it was delightful to revisit the whimsical stateliness of that particular common room." Lewis also wrote, "I did really have a very good evening the night before last when I exercised for the first time my newly acquired right of dining at Univ.—an exercise which must be rare because it is so damned expensive."[47] Interaction between Lewis and Poynton would be rather uncommon after this.

Philosophy Tutor E. F. Carritt

After Lewis completed Honour Moderations, he turned to *Literae Humaniores*, i.e., philosophy and ancient history. His philosophy tutor at Univ. was E. F. Carritt. Lewis came to rely on Carritt's instruction, advice, letters of recommendation, and friendship. When Lewis became a theist and later a Christian, they parted ways spiritually but remained friends.

---

[44] Lewis, *All My Road Before Me*, 329.
[45] Lewis, *All My Road Before Me*, 329.
[46] Entry of 19 February 1925, in Lewis, *All My Road Before Me*, 354.
[47] Letter of 23 February 1928, in Lewis, *Collected Letters*, 1:747.

Much later, even during a disagreement over the nature and purpose of culture, Lewis remained cordial and respectful toward his former tutor and took the high road in maintaining the friendship rather than distancing himself from his kind and generous tutor.

Edgar Frederick Carritt was born in London to Frederick Blasson Carritt, a London solicitor, and Edith Price on 27 February 1876. After studying at Bradfield College, a prep school in Berkshire County, he earned a scholarship to Hertford College in 1894.[48] At Hertford, Carritt earned a second in Honour Moderations under Tutor William Ralph Inge[49] and a first-class degree in Greats under philosophers Harold Prichard and Cook Wilson.[50]

E. F. Carritt, 1904
(Used by permission of the Master and Fellows of University College)

Carritt was elected a Fellow of Univ. in October 1898, soon after the completion of his degree, and he was admitted as a Fellow to teach philosophy on 20 April 1899.[51] The delay between his election and beginning to teach enabled Carritt to spend some months in early 1899 in Munich, Germany, where he lived with Professor Furtwängler and learned German (he was even more fluent in French and Italian), learning German mostly from the professor's son Willie Furtwängler, later a famous conductor.[52] Carritt specialized in aesthetics, moral philosophy (ethics), and political philosophy. A family friend, Cecil Torr, took him to Italy around the turn of the century and enabled him to develop an appreciation for the visual arts that had begun previously during an undergraduate visit to Paris. The cities he especially enjoyed were Florence, Venice, Siena, Palermo, and Rome.[53]

---

[48] Carritt, *Fifty Years a Don*, 1.
[49] Carritt, *Fifty Years a Don*, 8.
[50] He earned the degree in 1898. Carritt, *Fifty Years a Don*, 9, 11.
[51] For the dates and events of this sentence I am indebted to an email from Robin Darwall-Smith on 13 December 2021. Credit also goes to the Master and Fellows of University College, Oxford, for this and other information in this article. Carritt indicates that the illness of the philosophy tutor Vernon Storr resulted in the unexpected teaching post at Univ. Carritt, *Fifty Years a Don*, 14.
[52] Carritt seems to have married in 1900, although that event and date are not mentioned in any of the sources I consulted.
[53] Carritt, *Fifty Years a Don*, 16-7. He also cites Lucca, Orvieto, Pisa, Ravenna,

Carritt was influenced by the Italian philosopher Benedetto Croce in the field of aesthetics.[54] Carritt called Croce "the greatest man" he ever knew in philosophy.[55] One of Carritt's former students, Canon Adam Fox, recalls that Croce's doctrine of art as expression was what impressed Carritt most.[56] Carritt and Croce met when Croce came to Oxford to lecture on Sidney's *The Defence of Poesie*.

Soon after he started teaching at Univ., Carritt was elected to "a small club inaugurated by Cook Wilson and known as the Philosophy Tea. We met weekly in term at each other's rooms or houses for the discussion of short informal notes or questions, and once, at each end of term, for dinner and a more formal paper." At those teas, Carritt especially enjoyed the interaction between Harold Prichard (whom he had studied under), H. W. B. Joseph, and Lewis's Magdalen colleague J. A. Smith.[57]

Carritt also attended the Philosophical Society meetings on Sunday evenings, and during one session he met Albert Einstein. He asked Einstein about the proposition that "if two moving bodies seemed to change their relative positions, one of them or the spectator must have really moved. He [Einstein] laughed and said: 'I don't talk about reality, only what I can measure.'"[58]

Among the many positions Carritt held during his tenure as Fellow of Univ. were Praelector in Law (1900-1907), Librarian (1906-1916 and 1919-1945), Praelector in Logic (1909-1920), and Praelector in Philosophy (1921-1941). He was a judge for the Newdigate Prize[59] poem and an

---

Naples, Taormina, Paestum, Pompeii, and Cefalu as lesser favorites. He and his wife later traveled to Spain on holiday and saw the Cathedral at Terragona, Granada, Avila, and Segovia, a trip that included the Prado pictures, apparently a reference to the Prado Museum in Madrid. Carritt, *Fifty Years a Don*, 19.

[54] D. D. Raphael, "Edgar Frederick Carritt, 1876-1964," in *Proceedings of the British Academy*, 51 (1965), 441. Croce, an Italian idealist philosopher (1866-1952) wrote, for example, a lecture entitled *The Essence of Aesthetic* (1921).

[55] Raphael, *Proceedings*, 445.

[56] Adam Fox, "Edgar Carritt," in *University College Record*, 4.4 (Oxford, 1964), 240. This remembrance of Carritt's life comes from an address given by Canon Adam Fox at a memorial service for Edgar Carritt on 26 September 1964.

[57] Carritt, *Fifty Years a Don*, 25.

[58] Carritt, *Fifty Years a Don*, 29.

[59] The Newdigate Prize was founded by Sir Roger Newdigate in 1805. The award is given annually for the best student poem at the University of Oxford.

examiner for Greats.⁶⁰ Because of the Second World War, his Fellowship was extended beyond 1941. Many likely candidates for faculty positions were actively serving in the war, so Carritt was among those who were asked to continue their university duties until the war was over.⁶¹

In 1924, Carritt spent a year as a visiting professor at the University of Michigan in Ann Arbor, replacing Professor Dewitt Parker, who went on leave.⁶² While in Michigan, he stayed at the home of Brand and Frances Blanshard (Brand later became professor of philosophy at Yale University).⁶³ Carritt seems to have been one in a series of visiting professors from England, the two previous being the Poet Laureate Robert Bridges and Ancient History Tutor E. M. Walker.⁶⁴

In Ann Arbor, Carritt taught courses in the philosophy of Plato and Aristotle and in aesthetics, courses that Parker would ordinarily have taught.⁶⁵ *The Michigan Daily*, which once described Carritt as "the leading philosopher of England,"⁶⁶ reported some of Carritt's early impressions: "The first impression, though expected, is still overwhelming. It is that of huge numbers, complex organization, sharp contrast of interests and standards."⁶⁷ During the year he played tennis and handball, and during vacation he visited New York, Washington, Philadelphia, Baltimore, Norfolk, and Toronto.⁶⁸ At the end of that year in Michigan, Carritt was joined by his wife Winifred. They traveled through the Rocky Mountains, Vancouver, San Francisco, Yosemite, Los Angeles, and the Grand Canyon.⁶⁹ Near the end of the school year, he delivered the annual Phi Beta Kappa address on "An Ideal of a Liberal Education," when he spoke about the importance of the Classics as the best introduction to philosophy. He also

---

⁶⁰ Carritt, *Fifty Years a Don*, 52.

⁶¹ Email from Robin Darwall-Smith on 13 December 2021.

⁶² Paul Buckley, "March Meeting" (27 March 1924 in *The Proceedings of the Board of Regents of the University of Michigan* (1923-1926). http://quod.lib.umich.edu/. Search for "Carritt." Accessed 14 September 2022.

⁶³ Carritt, *Fifty Years a Don*, 44.

⁶⁴ Carritt, *Fifty Years a Don*, 44.

⁶⁵ *The Michigan Daily*, "Oxford Professor to Teach Here Next Year," 4 April 1924, 8.

⁶⁶ *The Michigan Daily*, "Carritt to Take Post of Parker Next Year," 28 March 1924, 1.

⁶⁷ *The Michigan Daily*, "Carritt, Visiting Professor from England, Astounded with Contrast between Life Here and at Oxford," 17 December 1924, 1.

⁶⁸ Carritt, *Fifty Years a Don*, 49-50.

⁶⁹ Carritt, *Fifty Years a Don*, 50.

stated, "I do believe that Plato is the most intellectually stimulating of all writers and his 'Republic' is the most educational book ever written."[70] He received an honorary membership in Phi Beta Kappa.[71]

In 1937, Carritt gave the annual Philosophical Lecture at the British Academy, an address called "An Ambiguity of the Word 'Good,'" reflecting on the work of G. E. Moore and H. W. B. Joseph.[72] His expertise in ethics probably explains why Lewis gave his first lecture at University College on "The Good, Its Position among Values."[73] In 1945, Carritt was elected a Fellow of the British Academy. His students remembered him as "clear and incisive, with a dry humour and no patience for rhetoric or verbiage but stimulating in the cogency and economy of his style."[74]

Carritt, a small, slight man, was unusual in other respects. Gilbert Morse, a college servant for Carritt during the 1930s, used to prepare ice cold bath water for Carritt in the morning, and Carritt would come downstairs in a large towel, leap into the bath water, and noisily wash himself. After about five minutes, the door of the bathroom would open, Carritt would emerge with the same towel around him, and he would run back upstairs, dripping water. After he had dried himself, Morse would have his breakfast ready and Carritt's day would begin.[75] In his autobiography, Carritt describes himself as "an enthusiastic bather" (swimmer), and he writes of swimming on the shores of "Aegina, . . . the Ilyssus, Tegernsee, The Blue Grotto, Dante's Fonte Branda, . . . a pool in Taygetus, besides many better known or nameless."[76]

Carritt read widely and he also loved art and literature. He combined philosophy with art and literature through his specialty in aesthetics. He was once seen by one of his students attending an exhibition of paintings, looking closely at every painting, since for him beauty was not simply a

---

[70] *The Michigan Daily*, "Carritt Addresses Honorary Society," 9 May 1925, 1.

[71] Raphael, *Proceedings*, 442.

[72] Raphael, *Proceedings*, 444. Horace William Brindley Joseph was the Senior Philosophical Tutor at New College. Lewis studied a text on logic that Joseph authored: *An Introduction to Logic* (1901).

[73] The date is 14 October 1914.

[74] Darwall-Smith, *A History of University College Oxford*, 465.

[75] Transcript of an interview between Norman Dix, college servant, and Peter Bayley, then English Fellow at Univ., provided in an email from Robin Darwall-Smith on 13 December 2021.

[76] Carritt, *Fifty Years a Don*, 20.

branch of aesthetics but something that he lived.[77]

Carritt desired especially to implant his interest in philosophy in his students. In a reminiscence of his former tutor, one student stated that Carritt "regarded every one of his pupils as an individual," adapting his methods in tutorials to the unique strengths and weaknesses of that student. "His pupils were to him, from the start, persons, and they soon became his friends."[78] This explains Lewis's closeness to Carritt. Like Lewis, Carritt also enjoyed rational opposition: "He rejoiced to find his most cherished positions under attack."[79] Carritt combined "great personal friendliness and intellectual rigour,"[80] two qualities that Lewis both appreciated and exemplified. Adam Fox described his writing as "lucid and often elegant without sacrificing the rigour."

Carritt enjoyed walking and talking, activities Lewis also enjoyed.[81] While the two men talked together, they never walked together. Carritt often walked with Launcelot Phelps of Oriel College, who later became Provost, in the countryside of Oxford. "It was Phelps' habit to walk up to twenty miles every Sunday, and for years he took me with him at least once a term."[82]

Carritt also knew William Archibald Spooner, the most well-known person in Oxford in his day, "more often quoted for his dry humour than for his genuine or ascribed mislettering ('You have tasted the worm; take the town drain at once')."[83] Another memorable character of Carritt's acquaintance was the President of Trinity, Rev. Dr. Herbert Blakiston. Once when Blakiston was preaching in the Trinity chapel by candlelight and having difficulty reading his manuscript, he read, "Some of you are frivolous of course. . . ." He then took another look at his writing, repeated the same phrase, and then stopped. After taking still another look at his

---

[77] "Edgar Carritt," *Record 1964*, 238-9.
[78] "Edgar Carritt," *Record 1964*, 238-9.
[79] "Edgar Carritt," *Record 1964*, 239.
[80] "Edgar Carritt," *Record 1964*, 239.
[81] Fox, "Edgar Carritt," *Record 1964*, 240. Carritt himself tells of his long walks on Dartmoor, often with Cecil Torr, in the Lake District, and in Skye. Carritt, *Fifty Years a Don*, 22.
[82] Carritt, *Fifty Years a Don*, 35.
[83] Carritt, *Fifty Years a Don*, 37. He meant to say, "you have wasted the term; take the down train at once." Sometimes called malapropisms or Spoonerisms.

manuscript, he stated, "I beg your pardon; some of you are followers of Christ."[84]

Upon his retirement in 1945,[85] Carritt was elected Emeritus Fellow and continued to write and teach philosophy. He was asked to serve as temporary Professor of Moral Philosophy at the University of Aberdeen for the autumn term of 1946 when John Laird, then Professor of Moral Philosophy, died suddenly.[86]

Carritt was beloved by his students, one of whom wrote, "He gave us an example of conscientiousness and kindness that could not fail to leave its mark."[87] Adam Fox and many other colleagues enjoyed that kindness at his home in Holywell and later on Boars Hill, when the hospitable Mr. and Mrs. Carritt welcomed them to their home.[88] In their retirement while living on Boars Hill, Carritt and Gilbert Murray often played tennis and took long walks together.[89] The poet Robert Bridges also became his neighbor on Boars Hill.[90] Carritt died at the age of 88 on 19 June 1964, in Ascot, England. He and his wife Winifred Etty were married for more than sixty-four years and had several children, none of them mentioned by name in his autobiography.[91]

Carritt was one of the first people to defend moral realism against A. J. Ayer, the premier exponent of Logical Positivism in the 1930s and 40s. Ayer wrote the major work on Logical Positivism, i.e., *Language, Truth, and Logic*, holding that moral claims are meaningless because they merely express emotions and therefore have no cognitive value.[92] Logical Positivism contended that only those statements that were empirically verifiable were meaningful, a position that rejected virtually all statements of faith, aesthetics, or ethics. Carritt's primary expertise was aesthetics and

---

[84] Carritt, *Fifty Years a Don*, 38. In the poor light, Blakiston misread the phrase "followers of Christ" for "frivolous of course."

[85] Raphael, *Proceedings*, 440.

[86] Carritt, *Fifty Years a Don*, 65.

[87] Raphael, *Proceedings*, 451.

[88] Fox, "Edgar Carritt," *Record 1964*, 238.

[89] Carritt, *Fifty Years a Don*, 69.

[90] Carritt, *Fifty Years a Don*, 71.

[91] "Edgar Carritt," *Record 1964*, 238. The name of only one child appears in the sources I consulted.

[92] Anthony Skelton, "E. F. Carritt (1876-1964)," in Hugh LaFollette, ed., *The International Encyclopedia of Ethics*, (Hoboken, NJ: Wiley-Blackwell, 2016), 1.

ethics, and he held that moral judgments and aesthetic conclusions were factual, even if not in a scientific or mathematical sense.[93] Carritt's position on moral realism probably helped Lewis in his defense of objective truth in *The Abolition of Man*, and the fact that Lewis later gave Carritt a copy of the book suggests further Carritt's influence.

Carritt held to what philosophers call ethical intuitionism, a branch of epistemology that describes how we form moral viewpoints, and he advocated aesthetical expressionism, the belief that art sought to convey a particular mood. Carritt authored many books in the fields of aesthetics, ethics, and politics (which he considered a branch of applied ethics[94]), among them *Theory of Beauty* (1914), *The Theory of Morals* (1928), *Philosophies of Beauty from Socrates to Robert Bridges* (1931), *What is Beauty?* (1932, an introduction to aesthetics), *Morals and Politics* (1935), *Ethical and Political Thinking* (1947), *Introduction to Aesthetics* (1949), *My Philosophy: Selected Essays of B. Croce* (1949), and *A Calendar of British Taste, 1600–1800* (1949).

Carritt Medallion by Hungarian sculptor Andor Meszaros

Among his well-known students were Adam Fox, whom Lewis knew as a friend, R. G. Collingwood, E. R. Dodds, Alec Paterson,[95] and, of course, Lewis himself. Yale Professor of Philosophy Brand Blanshard, who regarded Carritt as his best friend in England and dedicated one of his books to Carritt, once stated, "We never saw quite eye to eye philosophically," words that D. D. Raphael called "a masterpiece of understatement."[96]

Lewis and Carritt

Lewis first mentioned E. F. Carritt in a letter to his father on 1 May 1920.[97] Lewis had just passed Honour Moderations under Poynton's

---

[93] Skelton, "E. F. Carritt (1876-1964)," 1-2.
[94] Skelton, "E. F. Carritt (1876-1964)," 5.
[95] Author of *Across the Bridges*, founder of the Oxford and Bermondsey Club, and later a prisons commissioner and reformer. Carritt, *Fifty Years a Don*, 60.
[96] Raphael, *Proceedings*, 442.
[97] Lewis, *Collected Letters*, 1:485. Lewis does not mention Carritt by name. Lewis and Carritt may have met before this date, since there is a possibility that Carritt was seeking students for Univ. who had been turned down by other colleges. See Arend Smilde, "Why C. S. Lewis did not become a philosopher," *Philosophical Notes 1924*,

tutelage and was beginning Greats, the study of classical history and philosophy. In that letter, Lewis wrote about his two new tutors in history (George Stevenson) and philosophy (Edgar Carritt). He thought Carritt seemed quite nice.[98] Lewis took tutorials with Carritt for approximately twenty-five months. At this time, neither man claimed Christianity as his creed, although Lewis's conversion to Christianity in 1931 seems to have created disagreements between them.

Lewis interacted with Carritt for three main reasons. First, in their tutorial relationship, Lewis wrote philosophical papers for Carritt. Secondly, Carritt gave advice and endorsements for summer teaching that could earn some additional money and for teaching positions that could end in a full-time teaching position at the university. Thirdly, they dined together, sometimes in a social setting but sometimes to feed into one of the first two options.

Carritt attended some meetings of the Martlets, the undergraduate literary society at Oxford University to which Lewis belonged, and he occasionally presented papers, undoubtedly because of his interest in literature, especially the poetry of Matthew Arnold which Lewis also liked.[99] As a philosopher he was looking "at" aesthetics, while the literary person in him looked "along" literature.[100] He appears in the minutes of the Martlets as an Honorary Member, the undergraduates being the regular members. We have on record six meetings attended both by Lewis and by Carritt, although there were probably more.[101] The first such meeting took place on 9 February 1921. Lewis, then the President of the Martlets, invited student H. L. Hopper to read his paper on Romanticism in Art. Carritt weighed in on the definition of the essence of art as the discussion followed.

Inklings Studies Supplement No. 2, (2021), 49, note 33.
   [98] Lewis, *Collected Letters*, 1:486.
   [99] Arnold was known for his rejection of the supernatural, including both miracles and the redemptive sacrifice of Christ. See also Lewis, *All My Road Before Me*, 188.
   [100] To look "at" something is to analyze it, while looking "along" something is to experience it. See Lewis's essay, "Meditation in a Toolshed," for an explanation of looking "at" versus looking "along."
   [101] Besides the two times when he presented a paper, we know that Carritt also attended on 12 February 1919, 21 June 1922, 6 December 1922, and 14 November 1940. Ref. MS. Top. Oxon. d. 95 (1919-1923), Ref. MS. Top. Oxon. d.95/3-5 (1923-1946): 122. This citation refers to the actual minutes of the Martlets, which are kept in the Bodleian Library.

Carritt presented a paper at least twice at Martlets meetings. In 1921,[102] he read a paper on "Minor Symptoms of Taste in the 18th century," followed by a discussion on Homer, Charles Lamb, William Morris, Jane Austen, and John Masefield. In 1924,[103] Carritt read a paper on Matthew Arnold, which Lewis enjoyed. Carritt claimed that Lewis gave him the idea for the paper.[104] At one of the meetings attended by both Lewis and Carritt,[105] both took the same side against another member, which is evidence that the two of them thought alike on this matter.

After Lewis completed Greats, the relationship between Lewis and Carritt changed. Their friendship seems to have blossomed, as Lewis relied on Carritt's support for endorsements to various teaching positions in Oxford. On a personal level, on 24 June 1922, Lewis cycled to Bradfield College[106] to see Sophocles' *Antigone* performed in Greek, a play for which Carritt had given Lewis a ticket. That Carritt gave Lewis this ticket shows the appreciation Carritt had both for Lewis and for his alma mater. This and occasional invitations to dine at high table suggest that Carritt may have been grooming Lewis to be a fellow realist philosopher at the University.

We learn very little from Lewis about tutorials with Carritt during his first year with him. Lewis only began his diary in 1922, and he does not mention Carritt by name in his letters until 1924 (although he does refer to Carritt occasionally by his role as tutor). Carritt was mentioned much more frequently in Lewis's diary and especially his letters during his second year of tutorials with Carritt, and even then, not very often until May 1922. From that point on, Lewis was very interested in Carritt's support for finding him tutorials from which he could earn income and a teaching position in philosophy. As stated above, Carritt's kindness was well-known, so writing those testimonies on Lewis's behalf came easily to Carritt.

---

[102] 5 May 1921. See "Chronologically Lewis" for this date. http://www.joelheck.com/chronologically-lewis.php.

[103] 4 June 1924. See "Chronologically Lewis" for this date. See also Lewis, *All My Road Before Me*, 328.

[104] They had talked about Matthew Arnold on 30 January 1923. Lewis, *All My Road Before Me*, 188.

[105] The meeting of 21 June 1922. Lewis, *All My Road Before Me*, 53.

[106] Bradfield College was the prep school attended by E. F. Carritt before Carritt matriculated to Hertford College. This school was famous then, and still is today, for its performance of ancient Greek plays.

Tutorials and Lectures with Carritt

None of the papers Lewis wrote for his tutorials have survived, although some may have developed into later published essays. Over the years, Lewis wrote papers for his tutorials with Carritt as well as essays for publication, especially in Carritt's specialty in aesthetics and ethics. Among the topics were logic,[107] the philosophy of Benedetto Croce,[108] philosophical books,[109] Carritt's theory of the beautiful,[110] ethics,[111] the "Promethean Fallacy in Ethics,"[112] the theory of potentiality, the "Hegemony of Moral Values,"[113] the work of James Stephens (which he was actually writing for the Martlets[114]), and many others. Most of the topics were a standard part of the Greats curriculum, but the paper on Croce was a special interest of Carritt's. Since we get few details on these tutorials—and most of the details come from the later period of his work with Carritt—we can only guess what other topics he wrote about, but Lewis must have written about Plato and Aristotle in that first year. In addition, Lewis also heard Carritt present papers on several occasions, particularly at the Martlets.

Testimonials

Carritt was Lewis's primary advisor for potential teaching positions, including fellowships he applied for at Wadham College, Magdalen College, St. John's College, and Trinity College. The first time Lewis received Carritt's help was to find some students he could tutor so he could earn some extra

---

[107] This took place on 11 May 1922. Lewis, *All My Road Before Me*, 33

[108] This took place on 17 May 1922. Lewis, *All My Road Before Me*, 36.

[109] The date is 9 June 1922. Lewis, *All My Road Before Me*, 47.

[110] This is noted in the unpublished portion of C. S. Lewis's diary in the entry for 25 February 1924.,

[111] On 6 April 1923, Lewis prepared a prospectus on ethics to show Carritt. Lewis, *All My Road Before Me*, 229.

[112] Including an ethical scheme which Lewis discusses with Carritt on 11 October 1923. Lewis, *All My Road Before Me*, 230, 296.

[113] This topic may have been addressed after his time of study with Carritt. Its first mention appears on 6 March 1924 when he read the paper to the Oxford University Philosophical Society. Lewis, *All My Road Before Me*, 298.

[114] Walter Hooper, "To the Martlets," in *C. S. Lewis: Speaker and Teacher*, ed. by Carolyn Keefe (Grand Rapids: Zondervan, 1971), 51.

money during vacation.[115] Just a couple of weeks later, he received a note from Carritt, who thought that Farquharson could get Lewis some work for the vacation. The note also mentioned an available Fellowship at Magdalen College, although it was not the Fellowship Lewis eventually won.[116] Later that month, Lewis biked over to see Carritt and talked about an opening at Wadham College.[117]

Then, on 17 June 1922, having just completed Greats a few days earlier, Lewis met Carritt in the library, subsequently also asking Poynton and Stevenson, tutors in the Classics and history, respectively, for testimonials on Lewis's behalf. Also, on 23 September of that year, Lewis went to the Union and wrote to the Master of Univ., to E. F. Carritt, and to George Stevenson once again asking for testimonials.

Early in 1924, Lewis bused into Oxford with Carritt's and Wilson's testimonials, an application, and an essay. He left that packet of materials at St. John's College, where he was applying for another position.[118] Apparently for this occasion Carritt wrote the following words about Lewis, words that Lewis cited in a letter to his father: "He has not only real enthusiasm for knowledge, as distinct from its emoluments, but an unusual originality in pursuing it on his own lines. He seems to me the sort of man who is most likely to do something that would justify endowment, though there are some who have directed their studies more immediately to its attainment."[119] Those glowing words show the high regard Carritt had for Lewis. That high regard seems to have been reciprocated, since Lewis had written about both Carritt and George Stevenson, "Carritt and Steve . . . I still think to be good fellows in their different ways."[120]

At a dinner the next month, Carritt gave Lewis the notice about the vacancy at Trinity, a Fellowship in Philosophy worth £500 a year.[121] Lewis

---

[115] This took place on 27 May 1922. Entry of, in Lewis, *All My Road Before Me*, 41.
[116] Entry of 1 June 1922, in Lewis, *All My Road Before Me*, 43.
[117] Entry of 12 June 1922, in Lewis, *All My Road Before Me*, 49. The position would have involved being a junior dean, one who enforced regulations at the college, which Carritt discussed with him.
[118] Entry of 21 January 1924, in Lewis, *All My Road Before Me*, 284.
[119] Lewis, *Collected Letters*, 1:618. Thanks to Arend Smilde for pointing me to this quotation and the next one.
[120] Entry of 21 March 1923, in Lewis, *All My Road Before Me*, 222.
[121] Entry of 29 February 1924, in Lewis, *All My Road Before Me*, 292.

was trying for every available position, especially in philosophy. The very next month Lewis wrote to Carritt for a reference, which he received a few days later.[122]

The most notable support from Carritt, however, resulted in Lewis's appointment to replace Carritt for one year, while Carritt taught in the United States. In late April, Lewis received a wire from the Master of Univ., Michael Sadler, asking Lewis to come to Sadler's lodgings on Monday evening, 5 May 1924, to meet with Farquharson and Carritt. That evening, undoubtedly at Carritt's initiative, Sadler proposed that Lewis take over part of Carritt's work during the next year, while Carritt spent the year at the University of Michigan. Only Sadler had the authority to make the appointment. Sadler offered Lewis a one-year appointment to teach philosophy, a stipend of £200 for the year, and the responsibility to lecture twice a week. With a full year's experience teaching philosophy, Lewis would be better positioned to impress potential employers.

A month later, on 9 June 1924, Lewis dined with Carritt in hall. They were joined by the Master, Michael Sadler. Lewis went with Carritt into the Common Room. Poynton and Carritt were among those present. In the Common Room afterwards Poynton rose to hand out the wine. Lewis was now in the club. He never left. Later Lewis went to Carritt's rooms where he received more information about his forthcoming duties during Carritt's absence.

Dining and Other Social Occasions

Thirdly, their relationship was strengthened by numerous dining opportunities and other social occasions, some of which helped with advice for a teaching position. For example, in June 1922, Lewis dined in the Senior Common Room with Carritt, Stevenson, and others. Carritt and Lewis got into a long conversation on the subconscious, with Carritt denying its existence.[123] Two months later, Lewis went to tea at the Carritt home at Boars Hill, a small community three miles southwest of Oxford. Carritt promised to criticize Lewis's dissertation if he sent it to him.[124] Again, two

---

[122] Entry of 5 April 1924, in Lewis, *All My Road Before Me*, 311.
[123] Entry of 14 June 1922, in Lewis, *All My Road Before Me*, 49-50.
[124] This dissertation was a paper designed to demonstrate Lewis's qualifications for a teaching position. Entry of 17 August 1922, in Lewis, *All My Road Before Me*, 87.

months later, Lewis received a letter from Carritt, inviting Lewis to come and see him (Lewis doesn't mention why or what happened as a result).[125]

Two months after that invitation, Carritt sought out Lewis and invited him to dine at high table early in the next term, an invitation which Carritt followed through on in late January 1923.[126] When Lewis attended that dinner, the conversation centered on the expressionist theory of art. After the meal, Carritt invited Lewis to his room, where they talked about books, art, Matthew Arnold, and Pearsall Smith. Carritt was surprised to find that Lewis shared his flair for Arnold's poetry. Given Carritt's reserved nature, Lewis was amazed how personal the conversation became.[127]

On 13 June 1923, the day before he began exams for English language and literature, Lewis dined in the Senior Common Room with Carritt, George Stevenson, P. O. Simpson, and the Greats men of this year. The conversation was personal as Lewis talked about a book he had not read, and Carritt kidded Lewis about it.[128] After tea on 25 February 1924, Lewis walked to College and left a note for Carritt, accepting his dinner invitation for three days later.[129] The relationship was more than cordial.[130]

On 29 February 1924, Lewis dined with Carritt, Farquharson, and others. After dinner they went to the Common Room. Carritt and Lewis then walked to Allen's home in Holywell for the meeting of the Philosophical Society, where they heard H. D. Ziman read a paper on "Some Heresies." Very likely by this time, Carritt was working out the details for his year in Michigan and sizing up Lewis as his replacement.

Then, on 8 March 1924, Lewis received a card from Carritt asking Lewis to dine on Monday to meet Harold Prichard, Philosophy Fellow at Trinity College.[131] Lewis accepted. Just five days later, Lewis once again

---

[125] Entry of 27 October 1922, in Lewis, *All My Road Before Me*, 127.

[126] This occurred after a Martlets meeting on 6 December 1922. Lewis, *All My Road Before Me*, 150.

[127] Entry of 30 January 1923, in Lewis, *All My Road Before Me*, 187-8.

[128] Entry of 13 June 1923, in Lewis, *All My Road Before Me*, 243.

[129] Entry of 25 February 1924, in Lewis, *All My Road Before Me*, 290.

[130] See also "Chronologically Lewis" for 15, 21, and 22 March 1923; 6, 11, and 26 April 1923; and 13 June 1923. Lewis, *All My Road Before Me*, 83.

[131] Carritt was anxious for Lewis to meet Harold Arthur Prichard (1871-1947), who was the Philosophy Fellow of Trinity College (1898-1924). Prichard was later White's Professor of Moral Philosophy (1928-37), and he was already well known for his *Kant's Theory of Knowledge* (1909) and an influential paper, "Does Moral Philosophy Rest on a

attended the Philosophical Society meeting. This time he heard Carritt read a paper on the "Moral Faculty." At this point, Lewis was planning on a career in philosophy.[132]

But this was short-lived. After his year of teaching philosophy Lewis was appointed to a fellowship in English. Nevertheless, Lewis kept in contact with his old philosophy tutor Carritt. On 30 May 1926, after an early supper and return to College, Colin Hardie took Lewis to Hertford College to hear Samuel Alexander at the Philosophical Society. Carritt was among those present.[133] Alexander was the philosopher whose book *Space, Time and Deity* helped Lewis make a distinction between contemplation and enjoyment, what Lewis called looking "at" and looking "along." Alexander read a paper on artistic creation, attacking Croce in the process, which probably didn't sit well with Carritt, who was a fan of Croce. Only one more recorded contact occurred between Carritt and Lewis during Lewis's pre-Christian years. In 1928, Lewis returned to his undergraduate college and dined at Univ. for the first time since leaving there. Poynton, Farquharson, Carritt, and Stevenson were present this evening, and they spent some social time together in the Common Room.[134]

Contacts in 1933 and 1937,[135] the former a dining occasion that included Warren Lewis at Univ. and the latter one due to an invitation of some sort from Carritt, rounded out the recorded contacts prior to a conflict between Lewis and Carritt in 1940, which will be described later. Lewis tells Carritt, "I should have loved to come," but he had to decline the latter invitation.[136]

Shortly after his retirement, on 19 November 1945, Carritt's last recorded contact with Lewis took place. The Socratic Club met at St. John's College with the topic "The Empirical Basis of Moral Obligation" by Dr. R. Eisler with Carritt as the respondent. Eisler stated that men have died

---

Mistake?" in *Mind*, 21.81 (1912), 21-37.

[132] Entry of 13 March 1924, in Lewis, *All My Road Before Me*, 303.

[133] Entry of 30 May 1926, in Lewis, *All My Road Before Me*, 403-4.

[134] Lewis, *Collected Letters*, 1:747.

[135] The former a dining engagement at Univ. on 23 November 1933, and the latter on 29 October 1937. See Warren Hamilton Lewis, *Brothers and Friends: The Diaries of Major Warren Hamilton Lewis*, ed. by Clyde S. Kilby and Marjorie Lamp Mead (San Francisco: Harper and Row, 1982), 125; C. S. Lewis, *Collected Letters*, 2:220.

[136] Lewis, *Collected Letters*, 2:220. The precise date is 29 October 1937.

for incompatible convictions and that the existence of truth is necessary to make thinking possible. The certainty of sanity was only possible in company. *Cogitamus* ("we think") was the basis of our morals. Lewis, then President of the Socratic Club, agreed that truth was absolute and that truth was the only absolute value. Carritt also agreed with Eisler that the general nature of obligation was discoverable by reason, that we have an obligation to seek truth, and that this search was for the good of humanity. He disagreed that all values are relative, in agreement with *The Abolition of Man*, which he had received from Lewis in the previous year. Carritt apparently believed in G. E. Moore's argument that good cannot mean "what is liked by me,"[137] in other words that truth is subjective. While this is the last recorded contact with Carritt, there were undoubtedly other contacts that do not appear in any diaries or letters.

"Christianity and Culture"

Lewis's relationship with Carritt was to be tested in a public forum within the pages of the journal *Theology*. In January 1940, nearly two decades after he had studied under Carritt, Lewis sent "Christianity and Culture"[138] to editor Alec Vidler for publication in *Theology*.[139] The essay reacted to articles published in the journal by British historian and theologian George Every and literary scholar S. L. Bethell. In an article for *Theology*,[140] George Every had implied that "'sensitivity' or good taste were among the *notes* of the true Church, or that coarse, unimaginative people were less likely to be saved than refined and poetic people."[141] Bethell's article, "Poetry and

---

[137] Stella Aldwinckle, MS Meeting notes and lectures of the Socratic Club, The Stella Aldwinckle Papers, Box 8, Folder 384, 1945, Marion E. Wade Center, Wheaton College, Wheaton, IL. These notes are extremely sketchy, and this paragraph provides everything that Stella Aldwinckle had included in her papers.

[138] Letter of 25 January 1940, in Lewis, *Collected Letters*, 2:332. The article "Christianity and Culture" was published in *Theology*, 40.237 (March 1940), 166-79.

[139] The complete story is told in my chapter, "Alec Vidler: C. S. Lewis Was His Permanent Opposition," in *No Ordinary People: Twenty-One Friendships of C. S. Lewis* (Hamden, CT: Winged Lion Press, 2021), 263-85, especially pages 269-72.

[140] "The Necessity of Scrutiny," *Theology*, 38.225 (March 1939): 176-86. Every also wrote for *Theology* in September 1940. See C. S. Lewis, *Christian Reflections*, ed. by Walter Hooper (Grand Rapids: Eerdmans, 1967), 28.

[141] Lewis, *Christian Reflections*, 13.

Belief,"[142] had started the exchange between Lewis and both Bethell and Every. Lewis then explored various writers to determine their perspective on culture. The New Testament, Aristotle, Plato, St. Augustine, Thomas Aquinas, Jerome, the Church Fathers, and Thomas à Kempis all seemed to warn about culture. Others, such as Pope Gregory and John Milton seemed to support a positive appraisal of culture. Some aspects of culture are neutral, and others contain abuses. In addition, however, some aspects of culture bring pleasure, and pleasure is one of God's gifts.[143]

Lewis describes his own pre-Christian longing as "spilled religion"[144] and aspects of culture both as potential schoolmasters[145] and roads into Jerusalem,[146] so he sees spiritual value in culture. Nevertheless, Lewis calls the view of Bethell and Every an "inordinate esteem of culture by the cultured. . . ."[147] He finds value in spending time in "the suburbs of Jerusalem" because those echoes of Christian truth point to God.[148] Good taste, however, is not one of the notes of the true Church; unimaginative people are *not* less likely to be Christian than refined and poetic people.[149] Lewis here champions the ordinary person.

The May 1940 issue of *Theology* contained a reply from both Carritt and Bethell. The two men—Carritt and Lewis—had had a long talk the previous month, probably about their disagreement in *Theology*. Lewis called it "a long and rather annoying talk."[150] Bethell, "encouraged by the

---

[142] *Theology*, 39.229 (July 1939), 24-35.

[143] Lewis, *Christian Reflections*, 21, where Lewis writes, "When I ask what culture has done to me personally, the most obviously true answer is that it has given me quite an enormous amount of pleasure. I have no doubt at all that pleasure is in itself a good and pain in itself an evil; if not, then the whole Christian tradition about heaven and hell and the passion of our Lord seems to have no meaning."

[144] A phrase he borrowed from T. E. Hulme and also used in his 1943 Preface for *The Pilgrim's Regress*. C. S. Lewis, *Christian Reflections*, 23, note 1.

[145] See Gal. 3:24-26 in the King James Version.

[146] Lewis, *Christian Reflections*, 22.

[147] Lewis, *Christian Reflections*, 12.

[148] Lewis, *Christian Reflections*, 24. Or, Lewis concludes, "culture has a distinct part to play in bringing certain souls to Christ. Not all souls—there is a shorter, and safer, way which has always been followed by thousands of simple affectional natures who begin, where we hope to end, with devotion to the person of Christ." Lewis, *Christian Reflections*, 24.

[149] Lewis, *Christian Reflections*, 13.

[150] Letter of 29 April 1940, in Lewis, *Collected Letters*, 2:410. By this time, Carritt's

candour and charity of Mr Lewis's exposition,"[151] disagreed with Lewis's definition of culture, finding both Aquinas and Augustine supportive of the notion of Christian culture. He also argued, inexplicably, that Lewis's position implied that there was nothing of value in culture. Lewis had stated the opposite. Bethel also disagreed with Lewis's position that salvation was an individual matter, rather than a church matter, and that Lewis needed to consider the unconscious materialism that exists in the church.[152]

Carritt's reply shows his disdain for Lewis's "puritanical tradition" of what he labeled "text-hunting in the Gospels."[153] The ethicist Carritt claimed that Lewis obscured the main argument, which was a moral one and what Carritt defined as the question of whether a creature who was heading to heaven or hell could afford to spend any time on the study of literature. That was not the issue. Carritt misunderstood and exaggerated. Lewis had merely objected to the suggestion that refined taste was a mark of the Christian.

Carritt stated that Lewis felt the values of European literature could be instructive and helpful in bringing people to Christ. Second, he claimed that Lewis argued that culture could have value in the life of the believer, especially in their leisure hours, but Carritt did not like the idea of spending leisure time with Shakespeare or Dante to move a person from self-centeredness to a God-centered perspective. He also did not like Lewis's two options: on the one hand, the salvation of souls and the glory of God, and, on the other hand, nature, which Carritt called "the crux of the matter."[154] Nor did he like the suggestion from Lewis that when culture conflicts with our service to God, we should set aside those parts of culture. Carritt's inability to understand what Lewis meant by "the salvation of human souls" misses the point, when he writes, "I can best, and indeed only, glorify God by doing my duty, which would include, if that is possible, helping others to do theirs."[155]

---

reply had already been written and was at the editor's, too late to be recalled. My guess is that the two men did not agree but decided to pursue it no further to neither man's satisfaction.

[151] S. L. Bethell, "Christianity and Culture: Replies to Mr. Lewis," in *Theology*, 40.239 (May 1940), 356.

[152] Bethell, "Replies to Mr. Lewis," 356-62.

[153] E. F. Carritt, "Christianity and Culture: Replies to Mr. Lewis," in *Theology*, 40.239 (May 1940), 362.

[154] Carritt, "Replies to Mr. Lewis," 364.

[155] Carritt, "Replies to Mr. Lewis," 366.

In a letter to his brother Warren, Lewis expressed his dismay about Carritt's attack. He was unhappy that the editor would publish a response from Carritt, a non-Christian, in a Christian periodical. Lewis compared his own position to Warren writing an article for a military journal and being attacked by a pacifist.[156]

About a week later, Lewis wrote to Vidler about publishing a response to Carritt.[157] He suggested that if articles in *Theology* must be prepared for criticism by unbelievers, then the character of *Theology* would change significantly. He did not complain, and he never responded to Carritt's attack (he apparently thought better of it), but he was unhappy with Vidler. He did not, however, cut off his relationship with Carritt, or with Vidler for that matter. Later that year, Lewis presented to the Martlets "The Kappa Element in Romance,"[158] with Carritt in attendance. A few years later, in January 1944, he gave Carritt an inscribed copy of *The Abolition of Man*, which Carritt read and on whose pages Carritt made comments.[159] Lewis later added his responses to Carritt's comments. Lewis's gift of *The Abolition of Man* was done out of respect and affection, and the two men remained cordial toward one another.

Carritt's comments in his copy of *The Abolition of Man* showed his support with only minor objections. He comments, for example, that aesthetic judgments are "so much less certain than moral ones."[160] Occasionally, Lewis agrees with a mild criticism from Carritt. The two men seem to have read one another's comments, not to highlight their differences but to understand this important book better and, perhaps, to enable Lewis to improve the next printed edition. The conclusion, no doubt, gave Lewis confidence that, having run the gauntlet provided by his revered tutor, the message was sound. Two men, both of whom enjoyed

---

[156] Letter of 28 April 1940, in Lewis, *Collected Letters*, 1:401.

[157] Letter of 8 May 1940, in Lewis, *Collected Letters*, 2:412. Then, in January 1941, Charles Williams's untitled review of *The Problem of Pain* appeared in Alec Vidler's *Theology*. Lewis's letter was later reprinted as part II of the three-part text reprinted under the single title "Christianity and Culture" in *Christian Reflections*.

[158] On 14 November 1940. Roger Lancelyn Green and Walter Hooper, *C. S. Lewis: A Biography*, Rev. Ed. (San Diego: Harvest Book, 1974), 62.

[159] The Marion E. Wade Center, Wheaton College, Wheaton, Illinois, owns this copy of C. S. Lewis, *The Abolition of Man* (London: Oxford University Press, 1943) and has a transcription of the notes by Carritt and those by Lewis. (LB41, L49).

[160] From my transcription of notes in *The Abolition of Man*, 10, The Marion E. Wade Center, Wheaton, Illinois.

rational opposition, would have appreciated the perspectives, even the disagreements, of the other.

In the December 1940 issue of *Theology*, Lewis presented "Peace Proposals for Brother Every and Mr. Bethell," claiming that there was very little disagreement among the three men. He did not respond to Carritt, and he stated that he regarded Carritt "with all the respect and affection I feel for my old tutor and friend."[161] The position Lewis had adopted in the March 1940 issue of *Theology*, he stated, was that "culture, though not in itself meritorious, was innocent and pleasant, might be a vocation for some, was helpful in bringing certain souls to Christ and could be pursued to the glory of God."[162] He agreed with Bethel and Every that the beliefs of the writer were often implicit in their writings, but Lewis still maintained that he did not want excellence in reading and writing to be considered a spiritual value. The three men had not been very far apart, so this conclusion settled the matter. Every and Bethel offered one more installment, which appeared in *Theology* in February 1941.[163] After this letter, Lewis, Bethell, and Every no longer exchanged comments.

History Tutor George Hope Stevenson

George Hope Stevenson was the ancient history tutor[164] at University College.[165] He was born in Glasgow on 25 July 1880,[166] the son of Hugh F. Stevenson, an East India merchant. He was educated at Glasgow Academy, Glasgow University, and Balliol College.[167] At Glasgow University he

---

[161] Hooper, ed., *Christian Reflections*, 27.

[162] Hooper, ed., *Christian Reflections*, 28.

[163] George Every and S. L. Bethell, "Mr Lewis's Peace Proposals," in *Theology*, 42.248 (February 1941), 112-15.

[164] Darwall-Smith, *A History of University College Oxford*, 465.

[165] The photo, seen below, is Color Plate 15, by F. H. S. Shepherd in 1934. It appears in Darwall-Smith, *A History of University College Oxford*, between pages 278 and 279. The Oxford Fellows of Univ. are shown in this painting in the following order: Back row: David Lindsay Keir, Ernest Ainley Walker, A. D. 'Duncs' Gardner, G. D. H. Cole, John Maud, Arthur Goodhart, and John Wild. Front row: Edmund Bowen, Arthur Poynton, Sir Michael Sadler, A. S. L. Farquharson, Edgar Carritt, George Stevenson, and Kenneth Leys.

[166] https://universitystory.gla.ac.uk/biography/?id=WH22106&type=P. Accessed 3 January 2023.

[167] Peter Bayley, "Obituary for G. H. Stevenson ," 2. Peter Bayley's authorship of the

earned the Master of Arts in 1900,[168] graduating with First Class Honours in Classics. Stevenson earned numerous honors at Glasgow University, including the Jeffrey Gold Medal for the distinguished student of Greek, the Cowan Gold Medal (twice; earned while "seated upon the Black Stone"[169]), the Coulter Prize, the Muirhead Prize, and prizes for Greek prose, Mathematics, Latin prose composition, Logic and Metaphysics, and English literature.

University College Fellows
George Stevenson, front row, second from right.
Second from left is Poynton, and Carritt is next to Stevenson fifth from left
Used by permission of the Master and Fellows of University College

Stevenson then matriculated at Balliol in 1900, where he earned a First in Honour Moderations (the Classics, i.e., Greek and Latin language and literature) in 1902,[170] a First in *Literae Humaniores* (classical philosophy and

obituary is likely, but not certain.

[168] Email from Katy Mackin, Archives and Special Collections Assistant, University of Glasgow, Scotland on 10 August 2022.

[169] The Black Stone is a slab of dolerite, now embedded in a chair, known as the Blackstone Chair, fashioned of oak in the eighteenth century with inscriptions of the names of the founders, the arms of the University and of the constituent college, the Royal Arms of Scotland, and the Royal Arms of England. Students were examined while seated upon the Blackstone Chair as sand flowed through a time-glass for twenty minutes. Email from Katy Mackin on 13 September 2022.

[170] Lewis, *All My Road Before Me*, 470.

ancient history, also known as Greats), the B.A. in 1904, and the Master of Arts in 1907. He was a member of the Arnold Society and the Brackenbury Society (a comedy debating society). His Balliol education focused on the broad liberal arts, including Latin and Greek grammar and rhetoric, logic, ethics, and geometry.[171] Stevenson studied in Munich from 1904 to 1905, lectured in Ancient History at Edinburgh University from 1905 to 1906, and, in 1906, he was elected to a Fellowship as Praelector in Ancient History at University College,[172] to teach Greek and Roman history.

During World War I Stevenson worked in Intelligence, first as a Signals officer (i.e., communication) from 1915 to 1917, then at the War Office in 1917, and in 1918 at G.H.Q. (General Headquarters), Le Touquet, France, about 44 miles south of Calais on the shore of the English Channel.[173] His service dealt with the interpretation, or deciphering, of coded messages.[174] During a lunch invitation to which Stevenson had invited Lewis, Stevenson spoke of the code interpreting experts, who, after some were weeded out as ineffective, were entirely classical scholars.[175] The study of foreign languages apparently prepared these scholars to translate, or decipher, messages written in code. He returned to Univ. in 1919. During his tenure as a Fellow, he was an Examiner in *Literae Humaniores* at various times and a member of the Hebdomadal Council[176] from 1941 to 1949.[177]

After forty-three years as a Fellow, Stevenson retired in 1949. He served as Estates Bursar from 1939 until his retirement.[178] Stevenson was a Fellow at Univ. from 1906 until 1949,[179] and he was named Emeritus Fellow upon his retirement. Stevenson was Lewis's tutor in ancient history for most of

---

[171] Email from Nigel Buckley on 28 July 2022, Balliol College, Oxford.

[172] Lewis, *All My Road Before Me*, 470.

[173] Ivo Elliott, *Balliol College Register, Third Edition, 1900-1950* (Oxford: Oxford University Press, 1953), 71.

[174] Lewis, *All My Road Before Me*, 31.

[175] Lewis, *All My Road Before Me*, 31.

[176] The chief executive body for the University of Oxford.

[177] For much of the first two paragraphs, I am indebted to the *Balliol College Register*, courtesy of Nigel Buckley.

[178] Darwall-Smith, *A History of University College*, 498. The story is told by those who remember Stevenson that G. D. H. Cole begged Stevenson to take on the job as Bursar to prevent Lady Janet Beveridge from getting the position. This is according to Frederick Yarnold and George Cawkwell.

[179] Darwall-Smith, *A History of University College Oxford*, 535.

the time between May 1920 and June 1922 when Lewis sat for exams in Greats. Lewis wrote about his positive first impressions of Stevenson.[180] In early 1921, Lewis wrote to his father that his "history tutor has handed me over" to Benecke,[181] so it appears that Lewis studied with Benecke for a short time, since he continued to learn from Stevenson until he took exams in Greats in 1922.

Stevenson wrote articles for *Companion to Latin Studies* and *The Oxford Classical Dictionary*. In his obituary, the *Oxford Times* stated, "He wrote several chapters for Volumes IX and X of the *Cambridge Ancient History* on Provincial Administration, the Roman Army, and the Civil Wars of the years 68 and 69."[182] In 1922, he wrote an article on Roman transport for a book called *The Heritage of Rome*.[183] He authored two books, *The Roman Empire* (London: Thomas Nelson, 1930) and *Roman Provincial Administration Till the Age of the Antonines* (Oxford: Basil Blackwell, 1939), which was well regarded.[184] As Peter Bayley wrote, "The virtues of his scholarship and writing characterized his life."[185]

Stevenson was known to his friends as Hope rather than George. In appearance, he was "tweed-clad, pipe-smoking," and the *Oxford Magazine* described the "excellence of his sermons in Chapel, and the delight of his company, conversation, and of his random comment." His teaching was characterized by "sympathy, honesty, verve, patience, fascination with

---

[180] Lewis, *Collected Letters*, 1:485.

[181] Letter of 21 January 1921, in Lewis, *Collected Letters*, 1:516-17. This seems to have been unusual, however, because Benecke was a tutor at Magdalen College while Lewis was a student at Univ. Furthermore, we find very few references to Benecke during Lewis's student days, so it seems that this was temporary. Perhaps Benecke's expertise was in a field not well known by Stevenson. Robin Darwall-Smith indicates that Stevenson was especially good at Roman history, as his published writings indicate, so he may have handed Lewis to Benecke for aspects of Greek history.

[182] *Oxford Magazine*, cited in Peter Bayley, "Obituary for G. H. Stevenson," in *University College Record*, (Oxford, 1951/2), 2.

[183] Lewis, *All My Road Before Me*, 28. The title probably changed, since a book by this title does not appear in any searches.

[184] Darwall-Smith, *A History of University College Oxford*, 465. R. Currie also praises Stevenson's book. R. Currie, "The Arts and Social Studies, 1914-39," in *The History of the University of Oxford*, vol. 8: *The Twentieth Century*, ed. by Brian Harrison (Oxford: Oxford University Press, 1994), 135.

[185] *Oxford Magazine*, cited in Peter Bayley, "Obituary for G. H. Stevenson", in *University College Record* (Oxford, 1951/2), 2.

his subject, modesty,"[186] all of it in his refined Scottish accent that was remembered for decades thereafter.[187] Sir Peter Strawson described him as "a dull tutor" with "a sharp wit." Others described him as "a bit old-fashioned," but "not a bad tutor."[188]

At the age of 71, George Stevenson died in his sleep on 5 February 1952, the same day that Queen Elizabeth II's predecessor George VI died. Stevenson was a man of integrity, a generous man, active in his local Anglican church, St. Margaret's, Oxford, and serving for many years as Church Warden.[189] He gave many of his books to the Univ. library and when the organ of the chapel at Univ. was rebuilt in 1955, that work was partly funded by a bequest from Stevenson.[190] He was married to Phoebe Maurice Wadsworth, the only daughter of barrister-at-law Samuel Wadsworth, on 4 July 1912.[191] Stevenson and his wife had one daughter named Helen.[192]

Tutorials, Homework, and Exams

The most common references to Stevenson by Lewis are those occasions when Lewis was attending Stevenson's tutorials or doing homework or "Collections" for those same tutorials. Collections were a set of papers which students wrote at the beginning of term, usually three hours in length, to determine how much they recalled from previous terms. This would enable each tutor to craft the term's assignments to that student's knowledge and ability. They also served as practice runs for the public examinations students would take at the end of their studies.

Lewis demonstrated great potential, not only through his First Class Honours but also in the quality and speed of his work. Lewis's diary is

---

[186] Bayley, "Obituary for G. H. Stevenson," 2.

[187] Email from Robin Darwall-Smith on 30 August 2022. He mentions Gwynne Ovenstone and Sir Peter Strawson as being able to recall fondly and imitate that accent.

[188] This memory is one of several collected by Robin Darwall-Smith and shared with the author in a document entitled "Informal Memories of George Hope Stevenson (F. 1906-49)." This is a remembrance of Sir Peter Strawson. In the same document, Prof. David Raphael described Stevenson as "a little uninspiring." The last two comments in this paragraph come from Frederick Yarnold's memory.

[189] Lewis, *All My Road Before Me*, 470.

[190] Lewis, *All My Road Before Me*, 477.

[191] *The Law Times*, 133 (20 July 1912), 298.

[192] Lewis, *All My Road Before Me*, 31.

littered with references to studying history for Stevenson. More than fifty times Lewis mentions assignments in Greek or Roman history, studying for history Collections, writing those same Collections, and the like, all of them referring to his work under George Stevenson. One imagines that the setting for Lewis's *Till We Have Faces*, a fictional story set in lands near ancient Greece, was inspired by the teaching of Stevenson. Most of the actual references appear in the last month before Lewis took exams in Greats.[193]

While Lewis was studying Greats, Stevenson often distributed and monitored exams. On back-to-back days in 1922, Stevenson handed out Collections, one a paper in philosophy and the other a paper in ancient history. After writing for three hours on 28 April (term had begun on 27 April), Lewis went home and prepared for Greek and Roman history Collections the next day. After the second set of Collections, Stevenson interviewed Lewis, which was the custom. The excellence with which Lewis wrote must have been the reason why Stevenson told Lewis after Collections that he must not work too hard and that he need not attend any lectures.[194]

At the end of Greats, Lewis sat for six days of exams, from 8 June to 14 June 1922. Students wrote two three-hour exams each day unless they were so proficient in translation that they could complete that task more quickly. On three of the days that Lewis did translation, he completed the work in about two hours. In the morning of that first day, he wrote a paper on Roman history (these essays included translation and essay writing on that translation[195]) and in the afternoon he did Greek and Latin translation. On the second day, he wrote on philosophy in the morning and Roman history in the afternoon. On June 10, he wrote on Roman history in the morning and translated Plato and Aristotle in the afternoon. Two days later, after having Sunday off from exams, he wrote a philosophical paper on logic in the morning and did more translation in the afternoon. On Tuesday he wrote a general history paper in the morning and translated Latin prose in the afternoon. On the last day of exams, he wrote a paper on moral

---

[193] Entries of 2, 4, 11, and 18 May 1922, in Lewis, *All My Road Before Me*, 28, 29, 33, 36, and 41.
[194] Entries of 28 and 29 April 1922, in Lewis, *All My Road Before Me*, 26.
[195] Email from Robin Darwall-Smith on 30 August 2022.

and political philosophy in the morning and translated Greek prose in the afternoon.[196] On 4 August, he learned that he had earned a First.[197]

The Martlets and Social Occasions

Like E. F. Carritt, Lewis's other tutor for Greats, George Stevenson was involved in the Martlets.[198] We know of three recorded instances when Stevenson attended the meetings of the Martlets, one of them as the speaker. In that meeting, Stevenson spoke on "Goethe's Werther and Iphigenia."

The next month, Stevenson attended the joint meeting of the Univ. Martlets of Oxford and the Pembroke College Martlets of Cambridge, and a few years later he attended again.[199] This demonstrates not only an interest in literature, but also an interest in the students he and other Fellows were mentoring. He undoubtedly attended many other meetings. His interest in literature and related arts can perhaps also be seen in his attendance at productions of the Oxford University Dramatic Society.[200]

When we think of a student's relationship with a college instructor, we usually think only of the classroom or tutorial experience. At Oxford and Cambridge universities, however, the relationship was far more than a purely academic one. Tutors occasionally invited students to tea or a meal, as was the case with Stevenson and Lewis.

Most of the social occasions involving Stevenson and Lewis occurred at the end of their tutorial relationship and in the years thereafter. In fact, we know of only one such occasion before Lewis took Greats to complete his bachelor's degree, a lunch invitation about a month before those exams.[201]

Lewis enjoyed other meals with Stevenson as well, four times in the

---

[196] Lewis, *All My Road Before Me*, 46-9.

[197] That is, First Class Honours. Lewis, *All My Road Before Me*, 81.

[198] For more on the Martlets, see my article, "C. S. Lewis and the Martlets," *CSL: The Bulletin of The New York C. S. Lewis Society*. 45.2 (March/April 2014), 5-10. Also published at the HarperCollins weblog at https://www.cslewis.com/blog/category/joel-heck/. See also Minutes of the Martlets. Ref. MS. Top. Oxon. d. 95 (1919-1923).

[199] The dates are 9 March 1920, and 4 June 1924.

[200] On 11 February 1925, Lewis wrote that George Stevenson had attended and thought the O.U.D.S. production of *Peer Gynt* excellent. Lewis, *All My Road Before Me*, 351.

[201] Entry of 7 May 1922, in Lewis, *All My Road Before Me*, 31. Lewis sat for exams in Greats beginning on 8 June 1922.

Senior Common Room, the last time as a Fellow of Magdalen College, and one more lunch at the Stevenson home as well as a tea.[202] One final piece of social interaction occurred when Lewis gave a copy of *The Abolition of Man* not only to E. F. Carritt, but also to George Stevenson and Owen Barfield.[203]

Employment

One of the most important activities of a tutor is to assist students in finding employment upon graduation. In Lewis's case, they also talked about finding some tutoring that Lewis could do prior to graduation simply to make ends meet in the Lewis household. Stevenson was one of the dons who wrote recommendations for Lewis. E. F. Carritt, Michael Sadler, Carlyle, and others did the same.

Stevenson seems to have been responsible to some extent for the initial contact between Lewis and Sadler, which, in the end, won Lewis a one-year teaching position in philosophy for the school year 1924-25. This initial meeting was different. A note from Stevenson informed Lewis that the Master, Michael Sadler, wanted to see him. The conversation with Sadler dealt with a possible career in journalism, doing a trial book review of Garrod's *Wordsworth*, and Sadler's desire to find a teaching or writing position for Lewis. Thanks to Stevenson, Sadler now knew about Lewis's talent and was prepared for the suggestion that probably came from Carritt to fill in for Carritt during the 1924-25 year when Carritt would be at the University of Michigan. When Lewis went to see Stevenson to thank him for arranging the meeting, Stevenson said, "I don't mind telling you that it will be a scandal if this College or some College doesn't give you a fellowship soon."[204] Stevenson was confident in Lewis's abilities, having seen some of Lewis's written work and having discussed the various readings Lewis had done for history tutorials.

---

[202] On 15 October 1922, he went to the Stevenson home. He had tea there on 8 August 1922. See Lewis, *All My Road Before Me*, 82, 119. For the Senior Common Room, the dates are 14 June 1922, 8 August 1922, 30 January 1923, and 23 February 1928. See Lewis, *All My Road Before Me*, 49, 82, 187, and Lewis, *Collected Letters*, 1:747, for the dinners in the Senior Common Room.

[203] This took place in January 1944. See. Lewis's copy of *The Abolition of Man*, kept at the Marion E. Wade Center, Wheaton, Illinois. Call Number LB41.L49 1943, Copy 1.

[204] Entry of 16 October 1923, in Lewis, *All My Road Before Me*, 273,

Lewis contacted Stevenson six times over a ten-month period between May 1922 and March 1923[205]—and probably more times that he didn't record in his diary—for a written testimonial or some advice about employment opportunities. For family reasons, Lewis had seemingly limited his options to Oxford or the Oxford area, since Lewis wrote of Stevenson, "He thought a job at Reading for a year would help me to one at Oxford and approved of my idea of taking a season ticket and continuing to live at Oxford if I got it."[206]

In Conclusion

Poynton, Carritt, and Stevenson tutored Lewis in the Classics, philosophy, and ancient history, preparing Lewis for a lifetime of teaching, speaking, and writing. While Lewis rated W. T. Kirkpatrick as his finest tutor, these three Oxford dons carried on a similar role, filling nearly every rift in Lewis's mind with gold[207] and enabling one of the most gifted minds of the twentieth century to have a greater impact than he could imagine. They did not hesitate to correct him or disagree with him, but such rational opposition did not lessen Lewis's respect for them and his appreciation for their excellent instruction and their friendship.

---

[205] Entries of 2 and 27 May, 17 June, and 23 September 1922; 22 January, and 22 March 1923 in Lewis, *All My Road Before Me*, 28, 41, 51, 107-8, 183, and 223.

[206] Lewis, *All My Road Before Me*, 51.

[207] When Lewis once wrote on a student's paper, "Load every rift with ore," he was encouraging the use of examples and quotations, inviting the student to read widely and incorporate concepts from that reading into his writing. Personal correspondence dated 31 January 2003, from F. L. Hunt, who took tutorials from Lewis in Oxford during the early 1950s. This quotation comes from Keats's letter to Shelley on 16 August 1820, evidently alluding to the Mammon episode in Spenser's *Faerie Queene*, Book II, Canto VII, stanza xxviii, "Embost with massy gold of glorious gift, And with rich metall loaded every rift," with the idea that Keats wanted to encourage Shelley toward a richly textured verse. Thanks to J. O. Reed for this insight.

C. S. Lewis and
The Personal Opinion Fallacy

Jason Lepojärvi

"Even today there are those (some of them critics) who believe every novel and even every lyric to be autobiographical."[1]

Introduction

Authors sometimes become targets of critics who mistake the views expressed by their characters, plot, or atmosphere for the views held by the authors themselves. Consequently, as authors begin justifiably to fear that the opinions expressed in their art will be equated with their own real-life opinions, many begin censoring themselves, thus reducing diversity of perspective and diluting vigor of expression. The present essay reflects on this particular form of literary misreading and its contribution to other literary maladies. This form of misreading is closely related to what C. S. Lewis and E.M.W. Tillyard called "The Personal Heresy" and what W. K. Wimsatt and M. C. Beardsley called "The Intentional Fallacy," but is distinct from both. I wish to position Lewis—or my argument about Lewis—as a potential, albeit partial, solution to it.[2]

---

[1] C. S. Lewis, *The Discarded Image: An Introduction to Medieval and Renaissance Literature* (Cambridge: Cambridge University Press, 1964), 213.

[2] I am extremely grateful to a number of scholars and friends whose thoughtful feedback helped strengthen this essay in both substance and style. Holly Ordway, Michael Ward, Rachel Haliburton, Nathan Schlueter, Brenton Dickieson, Rebecca Sandberg, Simon Howard, and three anonymous readers—thank you.

I begin with a brief account of the epistolary literary disagreement between Lewis and E.M.W. Tillyard that took place over the course of three years in the mid-1930s, and which was then published by Oxford University Press as a co-authored book called *The Personal Heresy: A Controversy* (1939). This backstory, followed by a brief overview of "The Intentional Fallacy" (1946), will allow me to delineate and develop the related but distinct form of misreading, which is my main subject. Literary heresies or fallacies are corrected or, better still, avoided by good guiding principles of literary judgment. And so, we must say something about the corresponding form of good reading as well.

These deliberations are followed by a case study in which we observe the literary fallacy and its correction unfold: Lewis's reading of Milton in *A Preface to Paradise Lost* (1942) seems conscious of both the fallacy and the need to follow a corrective principle of literary judgment, without giving a name to either though describing both. Lewis's example is chosen simply to illustrate an argument, not to pronounce judgement on his overall literary prowess. Finally, to correct a number of possible misunderstandings about *my* argument, I conclude with some thoughts of further clarification. For reasons that relate to both the nature of imaginative literature and to Lewis as a writer, readers and critics of Lewis are particularly susceptible to what in this essay is called The Personal Opinion Fallacy.

The Personal Heresy and The Intentional Fallacy

Let us begin with *The Personal Heresy*. At the time of their literary dispute, C. S. Lewis (1898–1963) was Fellow of English Literature at Magdalen College, Oxford, and E.M.W. Tillyard (1889–1962) was Fellow of English Literature at Jesus College, Cambridge. Both men conducted themselves with thoroughness and charm, taking turns answering letters, three apiece. The first half of the debate played out in the pages of the journal *Essays and Studies* in 1934–1936. *The Personal Heresy* (1939) included three additional essays, a Preface from both authors, and a concluding note from Lewis. The publication was heralded by a live debate in Oxford on 7 February 1939.[3]

---

[3] C. S. Lewis, *The Collected Letters of C. S. Lewis*, ed. by Walter Hooper, 3 vols. (San Francisco: HarperCollins, 2004–7), 2:248, n. 24. Hereafter abbreviated *CL*.

The name of the heresy was first coined by Lewis in his opening letter which dramatically ends with an invitation "to be free of the personal heresy."[4] What was the disagreement about? In Lewis's words, the personal heresy is the proposition or belief—which he has taken from Tillyard—"that all poetry is *about* the poet's state of mind"[5] or, as Lewis says elsewhere, "the assumption that the writer's psychological state always flows unimpeded and undisguised into the product"[6] and that the primary task of reading poetry well is about gauging and connecting with *the poet's personality or state of mind*. This is the personal heresy. Lewis calls it "a serious error."[7]

Without going into the details of Lewis's many objections to this proposition or assumption, his objections did have an impact on Tillyard. Lewis's "probings," he writes in reply, "reveal what was unsound" and "helped me to mend my thoughts."[8] Tillyard's continued attempts to defend his view by refining the meaning of "personality" more carefully were met with Lewis's riposte, "glaring *petitio*"[9]: whether personality means the poet's "state of mind" (86), his "mental pattern," his "feelings,"[10] or what not, begs the question, exclaimed Lewis. Is poetry really about the poet's personality?

At several points in their disagreement, Tillyard uses superlatives to describe the profession of poetry. "The great poet" is a "superior person" unfavorably contrasted with "the ordinary man."[11] Lewis objects to this "false exaltation of poetry" or "Poetolatry,"[12] as he calls it. "One of my chief grievances against the Personal Heresy and its inevitable attendant Poetolatry," he says, "is the disparagement of common things and common men which they induce."[13] So, elitism is bad, but the denigration of the ordinary is worse. Lewis bemoans "the arrogance of poets"[14] and lets

---

[4] C. S. Lewis and E.M.W. Tillyard, *The Personal Heresy: A Controversy* (Oxford: Oxford University Press, 1939), 5, 35.

[5] Lewis and Tillyard, *Heresy*, 3.

[6] C. S. Lewis, "On Criticism," in *C. S. Lewis: Essay Collection and Other Short Pieces*, ed. by Lesley Walmsley (London: HarperCollins, 2000), 539–50, here 547.

[7] Lewis and Tillyard, *Heresy*, 5.
[8] Lewis and Tillyard, *Heresy*, 89.
[9] Lewis and Tillyard, *Heresy*, 67.
[10] Lewis and Tillyard, *Heresy*, 89.
[11] Lewis and Tillyard, *Heresy*, 99, 109.
[12] Lewis and Tillyard, *Heresy*, 119, 127–28.
[13] Lewis and Tillyard, *Heresy*, 119.
[14] Lewis and Tillyard, *Heresy*, 129.

loose: "Courtesy to our contemporaries must not forbid us to point out that a poet, an admitted and unmistakable poet, is sometimes (in certain periods, often) a man inferior to the majority in 'tenderness', 'enthusiasm', and 'knowledge of human nature'—not to speak of information, common-sense, fortitude, and courtesy. . . . Wash their feet, and I will praise your humility: sit at their feet, and you will be a fool."[15]

Most scholars, but not all, score the disagreement in Lewis's favor. Readers can judge for themselves. Mark Neal and Jerry Root say the problem with the heresy is that it "takes the reader's attention away from the text itself to focus on the author."[16] Jerry L. Daniel is thinking of Tillyard's camp when he says that "Many critics use the text before them as raw material to supply clues to the psychological state of the author."[17] To identify the poem with the poet, he says, is a kind of "crude biographical correspondence theory."[18] The reverse heresy, from the author's point of view, is literary self-expression, something that Lewis also deplored. "Self-expression is the personal heresy through the other end of the telescope."[19]

W. K. Wimsatt and M. C. Beardsley's seminal essay "The Intentional Fallacy" (1946) opens with invoking "*The Personal Heresy*, between Professors Lewis and Tillyard,"[20] signaling that the fallacy they want to discuss in this essay is relevant to, or perhaps even directly inspired by, Lewis and Tillyard's disagreement. Wimsatt and Beardsley's main argument is "that the design or intention of the author is neither *available* nor *desirable* as a standard for judging the success of a work of literary art."[21] The Intentional Fallacy is to assume the opposite: that the intention of the author *is* available and desirable as a standard of evaluation. And by intention they mean the "design or plan in the author's mind."[22]

The authors explain the critic's predicament: "One must ask how

---

[15] Lewis and Tillyard, *Heresy*, 130.

[16] Mark Neal and Jerry Root, *The Neglected C. S. Lewis: Exploring the Riches of His Most Overlooked Books* (Brewster, MA: Paraclete Press, 2020), 34.

[17] Jerry L. Daniel, "The Taste of the Pineapple," in *The Taste of the Pineapple: Essays on C. S. Lewis as Reader, Critic, and Imaginative Writer*, ed. by Bruce L. Edwards (Bowling Green, OH: Bowling Green State University Popular Press, 1988), 9–27, here 17.

[18] Daniel, "Pineapple," 31.

[19] Daniel, "Pineapple," 23.

[20] W. K. Wimsatt and M. C. Beardsley, "The Intentional Fallacy," in *The Sewanee Review*, 53.3 (1946), 468–88, here 468.

[21] Wimsatt and Beardsley, "Fallacy," 468, emphasis added.

[22] Wimsatt and Beardsley, "Fallacy," 469.

a critic expects to get an answer to the question about intention. How is he to find out what the poet tried to do? *If the poet succeeded in doing it, then the poem itself shows what he was trying to do.* And if the poet did not succeed, then the poem is not adequate evidence, and the critic must go outside the poem—for evidence of an intention that did not become effective in the poem."[23] I have highlighted the sentence that introduces a circular argument, a problem that is not entirely resolved in the remainder of the paper. The important distinction between an author's "intention" and a poem's "meaning" also remains somewhat underdeveloped or almost collapses.

To the best of my knowledge, there is no record of Lewis ever reading this essay by his two American colleagues in English Literature. Lewis's later essay "On Criticism," however, explicitly discusses an author's "intention," which is more carefully delineated from a text's "meaning." Lewis explains: "It is the author who *intends*; the book *means*."[24] His working definition of the author's intention in this essay is "that which, if it is realized, will in his eyes constitute success."[25] And the meaning of a text is "the series or system of emotions, reflections, and attitudes produced by reading it."[26]

> Of a book's meaning, in this sense, its author is not necessarily the best, and is never a perfect, judge. One of his intentions usually was that it should have a certain meaning: he cannot be sure that it has. He cannot even be sure that the meaning he intended it to have was in every way, or even at all, better than the meaning which readers find it in. Here, therefore, the critic has great freedom to range without fear of contradiction from the author's superior knowledge.[27]

This, the penultimate paragraph of Lewis's essay, almost reads like a charitable summary of or response to "The Intentional Fallacy." In any case, whether or not Lewis was aware of Wimsatt and Beardsley's essay, together all three inspired a generation of New Critics who contributed to the so-called "death of the author" movement in mid- and late-twentieth century literary criticism.

Readers might wonder about the difference between the conceptions

---

[23] Wimsatt and Beardsley, "Fallacy," 469.
[24] Lewis, "On Criticism," 549.
[25] Lewis, "On Criticism," 549.
[26] Lewis, "On Criticism," 549.
[27] Lewis, "On Criticism," 550.

of "heresy" and "fallacy," as I have been using them more or less interchangeably. Lewis and Tillyard could have equally titled their book *The Personal Fallacy* and Wimsatt and Beardsley their essay "The Intentional Heresy." It is largely a matter of taste. But a distinction can be made. "Heresy" concerns a problem with *belief*, while "fallacy" concerns a problem with patterns of *reasoning*. They can be seen as distinct but very closely related aspects of the same problem: the mistaken *belief* leads to the problematic *reasoning*. Lewis and Tillyard and Wimsatt and Beardsley are talking about two different forms of misreading, but both forms pertain at once to *belief* ("heresy") and *reasoning* ("fallacy").

Some readers or critics may embody the first aspect, others the second, and some both; but they seem slightly different in orientation and in how we might respond to them. If the source problem is one of mere *reasoning* ("fallacy"), the person making the case ought to be responsive to counterarguments; if the problem is one of *belief* ("heresy"), however, argument may prove less effective. It is easier to counter a deficiency in *reasoning* (for example, "the professor assigned to her students Plato's *The Republic* that has problematic views about gender, so the professor herself must subscribe to these views") when it is accidental and not necessarily rooted in *belief* (for example, "professors ought to assign only inoffensive readings they thoroughly agree with").

Before we move on to The Personal Opinion Fallacy (or Heresy) in the next section, we must make another porous distinction, that between two kinds of literature. Explicitly, both pairs of authors (Lewis and Tillyard, and Wimsatt and Beardsley) based their arguments almost exclusively on poetry. But it is clear that they believe the disagreement is about much more than this. It is about all "imaginative literature," as Lewis calls it, that is, "about poetry, drama, and the novel."[28] Elsewhere Lewis tells us that in the sixteenth century "poet" always "meant all imaginative writers"[29] and we can safely assume that Lewis retained some of this discarded broad use of the term. For our purposes, we may call this kind or form of writing *imaginative literature*. In Lewis's mind, this includes "verse or prose, short story, novel, play or what not."[30]

---

[28] Lewis and Tillyard, *Heresy*, 73.
[29] C. S. Lewis, "Sometimes Fairy Stories Say Best What's To Be Said," in *Lewis: Essay Collection and Other Pieces*, ed. by Lesley Walmsley, 526–8, here 526.
[30] Lewis, "Fairy Stories," 526.

In *The Personal Heresy* Lewis explains that the "most characteristic contents of [such] literary utterances are stories—accounts of events that did not take place."[31] In his essay "On Stories" (1947), which is basically the seed that would later grow into his book *An Experiment in Criticism* (1961), he distinguishes between the "fairy-tale" and the "realistic novel"[32] but both belong to the same genus of imaginative literature. This type of literature is not, he thinks, valuable for any impressions or expressions of the writer's personality, however defined.

The second type or form of literature, however, is different. This type of literature *is* more valuable for such purposes and beyond. This is implicit in what Lewis calls "truly personal writings."[33] We may call them *biographical literature* in contrast to imaginative literature. What, then, does biographical literature consist of? We may agree with Lewis that "[p]rivate letters are obviously in this class: and many essays," as he writes.[34] In short, everything that falls under what Lewis calls "historical data."[35] Similarly, Wimsatt and Beardsley speak of "biographical evidence."[36] This includes "journals, for example, or letters or reported conversations" and "notes."[37] The poet's own commentary about specific lines might be "taken more seriously . . . when off guard in a note."[38]

Of course, there are "borderline cases," as Lewis admits.[39] But this should not trouble us. The border between the *hill* and the *dale* is not easily categorized, but the categories of hill and dale remain distinct and comprehensible. Upon closer inspection some hills turn out to be mole-hills, just as some personal histories are shown to be imaginative fabrications, and vice versa. When this happens, when there is doubt about which is which, the solution, Lewis says in *An Experiment in Criticism*, is not the total abandonment of either but to "seek information from more

---

[31] Lewis and Tillyard, *Heresy*, 146.
[32] C. S. Lewis, *An Experiment in Criticism* (Cambridge: Cambridge University Press, 1961), 99.
[33] Lewis and Tillyard, *Heresy*, 73.
[34] Lewis and Tillyard, *Heresy*, 73.
[35] Lewis and Tillyard, *Heresy*, 76.
[36] Wimsatt and Beardsley, "Fallacy," 478.
[37] Wimsatt and Beardsley, "Fallacy," 478, 483.
[38] Wimsatt and Beardsley, "Fallacy," 485.
[39] Lewis and Tillyard, *Heresy*, 73.

reliable sources."[40] More will be said about this approach below.

With these preliminary thoughts in place, we may now begin to define the outlines of The Personal Opinion Fallacy and distinguish it from The Personal Heresy and The Intentional Fallacy. Lewis goes a long way toward describing it in various sources, but neither names it nor defines it.

The Personal Opinion Fallacy

The Personal Heresy, The Intentional Fallacy, and The Personal Opinion Fallacy, I propose, are three *species* of the same *genus* of misreading, which could be called Autobiographical Fallacies (or Heresies). This family of misreadings includes forms of misreading that treat "fictions as sources of knowledge"[41] in a wrong or incomplete way. They confuse life with art in some manner.

As noted above, The Personal Heresy uses imaginative literature primarily as raw material for clues to the author's *personality*. Perhaps it should have been called "The Personal*ity* Heresy" to make this clear. An example of this is when Lewis speaks of "the assumed, and [usually] concealed, major premise that the cynicism or disillusionment put into the mouths of some Shakespearian characters are Shakespeare's."[42] Cynicism is a personality trait. Personality traits, combined, a personality make. "It is sometimes asked," Lewis says, "whether Shakespeare was like this or that character in his plays."[43] He replies: "I do not know the answer."[44] Why not? We will get to this.

The Personal Opinion Fallacy, however, concerns specifically the author's *opinions*, not their personality. It is a parallel form of misreading, of gleaning biography from fiction in a somewhat deficient way. In its crudest form, The Personal Opinion Fallacy says in effect: "Because the story's character says this-or-that, or the plot or atmosphere or passage suggests this-or-that, the author must also personally think this-or-that." Such a disastrous interpretative premise cannot lead to valuable conclusions except by chance.

---

[40] Lewis, *Experiment*, 75.
[41] Lewis, *Experiment*, 75.
[42] Lewis and Tillyard, *Heresy*, 4.
[43] Lewis and Tillyard, *Heresy*, 74.
[44] Lewis and Tillyard, *Heresy*, 74.

The Intentional Fallacy, in slight contrast, concerns neither the personality nor the opinions of the *author* per se, but rather judgments about the meaning of *the text of imaginative literature*. Whereas The Personal Heresy and The Personal Opinion Fallacy argue from text to author, The Intentional Fallacy argues from author to text. Wimsatt and Beardsley argue that one should not interpret an imaginative text through the lens of non-textual authorial information; The Intentional Fallacy violates this principle. Lewis argues that one should be careful not to attribute to an author psychological states that are found in an imaginative text; The Personal Heresy violates this principle. Replace *psychological states* with *opinions*, and the same dynamic applies to The Personal Opinion Fallacy, too.

Fiction in particular is vulnerable to The Personal Opinion Fallacy by its very nature. This is chiefly because, as Lewis says, "[m]ost of the imaginative literature in the world is story-telling"[45] and, as we know, story-telling includes a lot of dialogue—that is, the exchange of literary utterances including opinions. So, no wonder that we are often drawn to consider these opinions. Fiction is also vulnerable to the fallacy because fiction is a mix of information, misinformation, and disinformation—or truth, mistakes, and lies. Lewis confessed to having learnt from novels in particular "a great deal of information" but also "plenty of misinformation."[46]

Lewis's own fiction is especially vulnerable. Much of his writing—on criticism, theology, and fiction alike—as one of his former students has said, "emerge from his pen not as distinct categories but as themselves mixed genres."[47] This is not a complaint. On the contrary, it speaks to what Owen Barfield has called Lewis's "presence of mind," by which he meant that "somehow what Lewis thought about everything was secretly present in what he said about anything."[48] This quality, said Barfield, "transcended all diversities of topic."[49] What, for example, is "the theme" of *Till We Have*

---

[45] Lewis and Tillyard, *Heresy*, 162 n. 2.

[46] Lewis, *Experiment*, 75.

[47] Stephen Prickett, "It Makes No Difference: Lewis's Criticism, Fiction, and Theology," in *C S. Lewis at Poets' Corner*, ed. Michael Ward and Peter S. Williams (Eugene, OR: Cascade, 2016), 186–97, here 189.

[48] Owen Barfield, "Preface," in *The Taste of the Pineapple*, ed. by Bruce L. Edwards, 1–6, here 2.

[49] Barfield, "Preface," *Pineapple*, 2.

Faces, my favorite novel by Lewis? A dozen suitable candidates come to mind. If I had to choose only one, I would place my money on love. What is the theme of The Cosmic Trilogy? Is it perhaps science, morality, lust for power, or gender?

Lewis's "presence of mind" and his evocative prose seduce the reader to treat everything as equally valuable source material for personal exploration but at the expense of a legion of possible misreadings and misunderstandings. In Lewis's books, continues this former student, "perceptions just jostle against each other, and are so interconnected that it is almost impossible to separate one strand from the next."[50] The philosopher Martin D'Arcy, a contemporary of Lewis at Oxford, said that so "absorbing" is Lewis's prose sometimes that "one's critical faculties are lulled to sleep."[51] The themes or strands of Lewis's fiction especially are numerous, interconnected, compound, organic, overlapping, diffusive; choose your metaphor.

As readers of imaginative literature, why should we avoid The Personal Opinion Fallacy? Why should we care in first place? Why bother at all?

Besides the peril of *authorial self-censorship* (in which the author might censor herself for fear of being interpreted incorrectly), another rather obvious but perhaps tautologous reason is that too often we end up falsely attributing to authors opinions that they perhaps did not in reality share. And this is an *injustice*, even if the opinions are "good," politically correct ones, but especially if they are not. Indeed, it is important to recognize that *both* prejudice *and* favoritism make us susceptible to this fallacy.

Lewis's unfinished and largely unknown essay "On Criticism," which made the helpful distinction between intention and meaning, is remarkable and relevant also because it concerns itself with "good" and "bad" reading of imaginative works specifically.[52] Lewis is speaking for all writers when he says that you can be "blamed and praised for saying what you never said and for not saying what you have said."[53] Undeserved approval is also "a

---

[50] Prickett, "It Makes No Difference," 192.

[51] Martin D'Arcy, "These Things Called Love," in *The New York Times*, 31 July 1960 (page unknown).

[52] "On Criticism" (see note footnote 5 above) was first published in its original draft form in *Of This and Other Worlds* in 1966. The text was probably meant as an address. It begins with "I want to talk about . . ." (Lewis, "On Criticism," 539).

[53] Lewis, "On Criticism," 542.

critical fault" just as much as undeserved blame, both being "critical vices."[54] Negative interpretations are, he says, "of course particularly dangerous for the lazy or hurried reviewer."[55] But apparently, "laudatory critics often show an equal ignorance of the text."[56] As exegesis, both are equally wrong.

But surely, we may ask, are not negative misreadings *morally* worse than positive ones? It is interesting that Lewis seems to disagree. He suggests that "fatuous praise from a manifest fool may hurt more than any deprecation."[57] I am reminded, for example, of his response to one of the few entirely positive reviews of *The Four Loves*, penned by one Anglican clergyman. It was, Lewis sighed in a private letter, "a prime example of the favourable review which exasperates an author *more* than the most spiteful censure could do. He misunderstands so deeply."[58] This is rather amusing, but I suspect this is hyperbolic. Certainly, as a rule, it is very doubtful. Rather, negative misreadings, I would suggest, are on average morally more problematic because of their possible ill effects—ill effects on ordinary mortal authors' feelings, reputations, and even livelihoods. Praise culture is not a serious malady; cancel culture is. But it is also a problem for the critic or canceler's own heart. Better to err in charity. We should avoid The Personal Opinion Fallacy because we care about justice. We want to be good people.

We also want to be *good readers*. No true lover of fiction often commits this fallacy. When we do commit it, it is as likely to reveal something about ourselves as it is about the writer. We might betray our own prejudices and biases, which we project onto others. Fiction is further vulnerable because "to a determined critic," as Lewis says in *An Experiment in Criticism*, almost "everything can be a symbol, or an irony, or an ambiguity,"[59] open to the most fantastical interpretations. "Thus increasingly we meet only ourselves."[60] This misreading is important because it interferes with our ability to judge and appreciate the literary work in and of itself and even because it moves us away from enjoyment and literary analysis into

---

[54] Lewis, "On Criticism," 542.
[55] Lewis, "On Criticism," 542.
[56] Lewis, "On Criticism," 542.
[57] Lewis, "On Criticism," 540.
[58] Letter of 3 June 1960, in Lewis, *CL*, 3:1156, emphasis added.
[59] Lewis, *Experiment*, 85.
[60] Lewis, *Experiment*, 85.

something like half-baked psychoanalysis. Identity politics applied to imaginative literature profoundly misunderstands the whole enterprise and damages or ruins imaginative literature and the moral imagination.

The Personal Opinion Fallacy is also a *disfavor to scholarship*, resulting in a colossal loss of academic energy. If left unchecked, false trails are blazed that might take generations to correct. In literary criticism, as Lewis says, "ideas still circulate from one critic to another which have obviously not been verified by actual reading."[61] This of course applies to all disciplines. When these ideas are damaging, their correction might feel (to the corrected critic or their admirers) like defensiveness or partisanship.

So much for what The Personal Opinion Fallacy is and for some reasons why we should avoid it. Next, I will turn to *how* we can avoid it. We can then look at how the fallacy and its correction unfold in a real example of applied literary criticism.

The Principle of Biographical Verification

Hints about the correction to The Personal Opinion Fallacy, the literary antibody to the virus, have been dropped throughout our reflections. But it will help to spell it out in more detail and give it a name.

We remember the question about whether Shakespeare was like this or that of his characters. Lewis said he did not know the answer. Why not? Because, he explained, "to decide that question we must *start investigating historical data* and moral principles."[62] In other words, if biography is what interests us, we must turn from imaginative literature to biographical literature (and, in this case, to ethics). We must ground our biographical speculations in biographical literature. Let history inform, and if necessary, tether theory.

This Principle of Biographical Verification, as we might call it, is an effective curative to The Personal Opinion Fallacy but also to many other forms of bad reading. In reading poetry, Wimsatt and Beardsley put it this way: "We ought to impute the thoughts and attitudes of the poem immediately to the dramatic *speaker*, and if to the author at all, only by a biographical act of inference."[63]

---

[61] Lewis, "On Criticism," 543.
[62] Lewis and Tillyard, *Heresy*, 76, emphasis added.
[63] Wimsatt and Beardsley, "Fallacy," 470.

An analogy might help to explain both the problem and the principle. Imagine a *black and white painting*, which represents an imaginative literary artefact, such as a novel. You see several hearts in either black or white. Both colors represent opinions. But only one color represents the personal opinions of the author. The other represents opinions expressed or suggested by the characters, plot, atmosphere, or specific passages, which the author may not personally agree with. Now, if we were asked to say which is which, we could not answer, could we? Why not? Because we lack contrast. We lack a *backdrop* against which to evaluate the content. In short, we lack what we have called *biographical literature*. Once we do our homework—once we read essays, letters, notes, memoirs, and so on—represented analogously, say, by a *black wall* on which the painting hangs, we will be in a much better position to sift through the personal and the fictional and to avoid The Personal Opinion Fallacy. We will then realize that the black hearts, and not the white, correspond more closely to the author's personal views. We might even begin to see some shades of grey.

Want to know which theory of atonement Lewis subscribed to, if any? Put down, for a moment, your copy of *The Lion, the Witch and the Wardrobe*—yes, despite Aslan's sacrifice—and pick up *Mere Christianity* or, even better, a copy of his collected letters.[64] Want to know how Lewis felt about teenage girls, about budding female sexuality? Put down *The Last Battle*—yes, despite Susan—and read his pre-conversion diary *All My Road Before Me* for his younger immature view or his later biographical writings for his more mature one. Or read memoirs of Lewis by women who knew him. We may then return to his fiction with clearer vision for thematic insight but immunized against reading too much into it.

Almost absurdly, Tillyard recognizes the merits of The Principle of Biographical Verification but regards it as a form of cheating. "Biography," he admits, "may substantially help our understanding of the mental pattern as revealed in his [the poet's] art."[65] But he likens "the mixture of biography and criticism" to "looking up the answer to a problem when tired of trying

---

[64] Even *Mere Christianity* has to be read carefully in this respect. It is not meant to be a window into Lewis's own theology, but an introductory overview of the Christian faith in general: getting people into the "hallway," as Lewis says, not into his preferred room labeled "Anglicanism."

[65] Lewis and Tillyard, *Heresy*, 52.

to solve it."⁶⁶ Lewis's proposal of turning to "historical data" *if* the author's personal information is what we seek from imaginative literature, he thinks, is actually the critic's "besetting sin" better avoided: biography is "an illegitimate short cut."⁶⁷ Far from cheating, I believe, it is the most basic and necessary work we must do if we are to be good readers, let alone good critics.

Sometimes, of course, even The Principle of Biographical Verification yields no definitive answer. When that happens, we may speculate and conjecture. But we must be honest. Again, Lewis offers a helpful supporting principle: "[I]f I hazard a conjecture, it must be with full knowledge and with a clear warning to my reader that it is a long shot, far more likely to be wrong than right."⁶⁸ Especially, I would add, if the writer or artist is dead and not around to refute us, or even if they are. This is also what erring in charity looks like.

Critical judgement is a difficult undertaking for both trained and untrained readers. This should instill in us humility and moderation. "How can we be confident," ask Neal and Root, "that we have understood the motives and intentions of others?"⁶⁹ This is a great question. Charles Williams, who made a living by reviewing books, wrote that "not one mind in a thousand can be trusted to state accurately what its opponent says, much less what he thinks."⁷⁰ The more significant or sensitive the questions or values being speculated about, the more unwise forgetting this guiding principle is. A responsible reader or scholar would not *too hastily* draw conclusions about any author's views on, say, sex, race, or religion, and so on. But to speculate about other matters might be less dubious. It is precisely when serious allegations are made that standards of probity should rise, not fall. Otherwise, we risk becoming tedious heresy-hunters of the latest shibboleth, taboo or sin; so eager to catch authors "off guard" that we only drop our own.

A perfect example of this is the way J. K. Rowling's feminist views on

---

⁶⁶ Lewis and Tillyard, *Heresy*, 52, 53.
⁶⁷ Lewis and Tillyard, *Heresy*, 52.
⁶⁸ Lewis, "On Criticism," 544.
⁶⁹ Neal and Root, *Neglected*, 49.
⁷⁰ Charles Williams, *The Descent of the Dove: A Short History of the Holy Spirit in the Church* (Vancouver: Regent College Publishing, 2002), 112.

transgenderism led some activists to attack her latest mystery *Troubled Blood* (2020) on the grounds that her "transphobia" was on full display because the villain sometimes dressed as a woman to lull his victims into a state of complacency. A rather standard murder mystery trope (how does the murderer overpower his victims) was then misread as a sign of the author's other beliefs. Similarly, John Goldthwaite cites the exchange in *The Voyage of the Dawn Treader* between Caspian and Lucy about the girl who squints and has freckles as an example of Lewis's "smug" and "snide" disparagement of girls.[71] Goldthwaite not only falls into the trap of equating characters' views with authorial views, but he also mistakenly extrapolates from the particular to the general. He would benefit from reading Lewis's letter to a young reader, Laurence Krieg, on 24 October 1955: "I don't dislike Panthers at all, I think they are one of the loveliest animals there are. I don't remember that I have put any *bad* panthers in the books (there are some good ones fighting against Rabadash in [*The Horse and His Boy*] aren't there?) and even if I had that wouldn't mean that I thought all Panthers bad, any more than I think all men bad because of Uncle Andrew, or all boys bad because Edmund was once a traitor."[72]

In the next section, I look more carefully at a case study in which we observe the literary fallacy and its correction play out. The book that had originally sparked the literary disagreement between Lewis and Tillyard was the latter's study *Milton* (1930). A few years after the closure of their "controversy," Lewis published his own study of Milton called *A Preface to Paradise Lost* (1942). In my view, Lewis's *Preface* is conscious of both the peril of The Personal Opinion Fallacy and the need to steer his deliberations according to The Principle of Biographical Verification, albeit without naming either the fallacy or the principle.

Case Study: Lewis on Milton

The opening sentence of *A Preface to Paradise Lost* invokes the intention of an author and the function of a literary artefact. "The first qualification for judging any piece of workmanship from a corkscrew to

---

[71] John Goldthwaite, *The Natural History of Make-Believe* (Oxford: Oxford University Press, 1996), 227–9.
[72] Letter of 24 October 1955, in Lewis, *CL*, 3:666.

a cathedral is to know *what* it is—what it was intended to do and how it is meant to be used."⁷³ The answer to the first, "what Milton meant it to be,"⁷⁴ is that Milton intended to write in the genre of epic poetry. The form determines much of the resulting artistic decisions. At the outset, Lewis draws a distinction between *logos* and *poiema*: "Every poem can be considered in two ways—as what the poet has to say, and as a *thing* which he *makes*."⁷⁵ As logos or something said a poem "is an expression of opinions and emotions,"⁷⁶ the owner of which is left undetermined.

Lewis also draws a distinction between a poem's Mother and Father. Every poem has "two parents—its mother being the mass of experience, thought, and the like, inside the poet, and its father the pre-existing Form (epic, tragedy, the novel, and what not)."⁷⁷ He would later elsewhere speak of the Man and the Author, respectively.⁷⁸ Lewis wants to focus on the Father (the literary Form) because, he says, perhaps with a nod to Tillyard, "excellent helps to the study of the raw material inside the poet— the experiences, character, and opinions of the man Milton—already exist."⁷⁹ Opinions belong to the study of the Mother (the author's "mass of experience," and so on). Interestingly, despite his professed paternal focus, Lewis has quite a bit to say about her, as well. Chapter XII on "The Theology of *Paradise Lost*" is particularly relevant and revealing.⁸⁰

In this chapter, Lewis divides the doctrines or theological teachings in *Paradise Lost* into four groups: "(1) those which really occur in *Paradise Lost*, but which, so far from being heretical, are the commonplaces of Christian theology; (2) those which are heretical, but do not occur in Milton; (3) those which are heretical and occur in Milton's *De Doctrina*, but not in *Paradise Lost*; (4) those which are heretical and do really occur in *Paradise Lost*."⁸¹ For clarification of the second set, Lewis means those which are heretical but do not occur in Milton's theological study *De Doctrina*: in

---

⁷³ C. S. Lewis, *A Preface to Paradise Lost* (Oxford: Oxford University Press, 1942), 2.
⁷⁴ Lewis, *Preface*, 1.
⁷⁵ Lewis, *Preface*, 2. The words *logos* and *poiema* do not appear in this work.
⁷⁶ Lewis, *Preface*, 2–3.
⁷⁷ Lewis, *Preface*, 3.
⁷⁸ Lewis, "Fairy Stories."
⁷⁹ Lewis, *Preface*, 3.
⁸⁰ Lewis, *Preface*, 82–93.
⁸¹ Lewis, *Preface*, 83.

other words, doctrines that Milton did not subscribe to personally. As for *Paradise Lost*, Lewis believes that heretical elements do, in fact, "exist in it, but are only discoverable by search,"[82] that is, by looking very carefully. The key words here seem to be 'in it,' as opposed to 'in him.' This leaves the question open: are the elements Milton's own?

In answering *this* question, Lewis turns from the poem to the theological study, from imaginative literature to more biographical literature. He is, in fact, following what we called The Principle of Biographical Verification. In doing so, sometimes his verdict is "I see no evidence that Milton believed in anything of the sort."[83] At other times, suspicions are confirmed, but "we should not from this passage, nor from any passage in the whole poem, have discovered the poet's Arianism without the aid of external evidence."[84] Such things are detected "only by the aid of external evidence from the *De Doctrina*."[85] Did Milton reject the doctrine of *ex nihilo*? This too is confirmed by turning to biographical sources.[86] "We know from his prose works that Milton believed. . . ."[87] An example of the third category (something subscribed to by Milton but absent in *Paradise Lost*) is Milton's genuine private political stance in favor of Republicanism. Lewis thinks critics who detect in *Paradise Lost* a private sympathy for Satan's anti-monarchical rebellion are mistaken for *literary* reasons. This is not a perfect example of The Personal Opinion Fallacy and almost its reverse mistake. Such critics begin by *already* knowing the author's genuine opinion and mistakenly detect it in fiction as well, as opposed to supposedly inferring a contested opinion from fiction.

At one point, Lewis seems to anticipate the charge that *he himself* might have committed The Personal Opinion Fallacy. He writes: "It may be objected that I have been treating the poem as a legal document, finding out what Milton's words strictly hold him to, and thrusting aside the evidence of his other works which shows us what he 'really meant' by them. And certainly if we were in pursuit of Milton's private thoughts and were valuing

---

[82] Lewis, *Preface*, 82.
[83] Lewis, *Preface*, 84.
[84] Lewis, *Preface*, 86–7.
[85] Lewis, *Preface*, 90.
[86] Lewis, *Preface*, 89.
[87] Lewis, *Preface*, 95.

the poem simply for the light it threw on those, my method would be very perverse."[88] Here perverse means lopsided, putting the cart before the horse; or, worse still, asking the cart about the horse while ignoring the horse! Perverse means neglecting The Principle of Biographical Verification.

Lewis goes even further than this. "Even the poet, when he appears in the first person within his own poem, is not to be taken as the private individual John Milton."[89] This would be "a gross error indeed."[90] This statement takes The Personal Opinion Fallacy to a further level of complexity and would of course apply to Lewis himself in such works as *The Pilgrim's Regress* or *The Great Divorce*—just as some philosophers have argued it applies to Plato *in persona* of Socrates and to the other characters in the dialogues who might have had real-life counterparts in Plato's circle of friends.[91] But why would it be an error?

Lewis seems to think that the answer is more or less obvious. Because "the real man, of course, being a man, felt more things, and less interesting things, about it [i.e. any given subject] than are expressed. . . . From that total experience the author selects, for his epic and for his tragedy, what is proper to each."[92] In short, no literary work can express the "total thought about all the subjects mentioned in it."[93] Experience and opinion can never be comprehensively squeezed into literature, least of all fiction. The error to guard against is the declaration: "Ah, so *this* is what Milton or Lewis or Plato 'really' believed about our subject."

Conclusion: "Things That Records Do Not Record"

I began these reflections with brief overviews of *The Personal Heresy* and "The Intentional Fallacy," and I proposed a distinction between imaginative and biographical literature. I introduced a related but distinct form of literary misreading called The Personal Opinion Fallacy. I discussed reasons why fiction in particular might be vulnerable to this fallacy and

---

[88] Lewis, *Preface*, 91.
[89] Lewis, *Preface*, 59.
[90] Lewis, *Preface*, 59.
[91] See, for example, Alexander Nehamas, *The Art of Living: Socratic Reflections from Plato to Foucault* (Berkeley, CA: University of California Press, 1998).
[92] Lewis, *Preface*, 59.
[93] Lewis, *Preface*, 91.

suggested some motives why readers of fiction might want to avoid it. The Principle of Biographical Verification helps steer the responsible reader away from seeing too much in literary works of imagination. Finally, I analyzed Lewis's reading of Milton in light of both the fallacy and its correction. Before closing, I wish to guard the reader against some possible misunderstandings of my argument.

I am not saying that imaginative literature, let alone Lewis's fiction, is free from personal opinions. On the contrary, it is often replete with them. Even in *The Personal Heresy* Lewis acknowledged that sometimes authors *deliberately* cloak their opinions and "put on the disguise of verse."[94] Certainly, *something* of the author's personality and opinions may be in evidence in their creation. I doubt anyone would deny this. In his short piece in *The New York Times Book Review* "Sometimes Fairy Stories May Say Best What's To Be Said,"[95] Lewis admits that *part* of his "motive" or "intention" in writing *The Chronicles of Narnia* was indeed to smuggle in theology, or, more precisely, the "taste" or "potency" or "meaning" of the reality behind Christian doctrines that he thinks have gone flat, like the teaching on forgiveness. My claim is not that writers never try to educate or influence their readers. Of course they do.

Further, I entertain no assumption that interpreting so-called biographical literature is always straightforward and unproblematic. It is not. Biography has to be read carefully, as well, that is, not always at face value. This is for several reasons. Authors misremember things. They change their mind. They dramatize. They conceal. They lie. Lewis was well aware of this aspect of biographical writing. Stephen Medcalf noted how in his autobiography *Surprised by Joy* "Lewis carried self-dramatization far beyond [ordinary] license" and "wonderfully mythicized his memory of his life."[96] Alister McGrath has said basically the same in his essay "The Enigma of Autobiography: Critical Reflections on *Surprised by Joy*."[97] If reading is

---

[94] Lewis, *Heresy*, 73.

[95] Nov. 18, 1956, 310. Lewis, "Fairy Stories," 527–8.

[96] Stephen Medcalf, "Language and Self-Consciousness: The Making and Breaking of Lewis's Personae," in *Word and Story in C. S. Lewis: Language and Narrative in Theory and Practice*, ed. by Peter J. Schakel and Charles A. Huttar (Eugene, OR: Wipf and Stock, Year, 2007 [1991]), 109–44, here 113.

[97] Alister McGrath, "The Enigma of Autobiography: Critical Reflections on *Surprised by Joy*," in Alister McGrath, *The Intellectual World of C. S. Lewis* (London:

difficult, so are introspection and retrospection. But all this belongs to a different set of literary problems. It is not the subject of this essay.

Finally, I am not saying that psychological theories are unhelpful in interpreting an author's life or letters. There are several decent examples of good, careful, and responsible ways to glean biography from fiction—or, I should say, in conjunction with fiction, back and forth between imaginary and biographical literature, with measured analysis of both. Medcalf's own essay is one of these examples.[98] Even when nothing in the biographical literature explicitly demonstrates or supports what we see, or think we have seen, in fiction, we just *might* be right, however improbable. But *proving* this is quite another matter and full of dangers. Lewis's essay "Psycho-Analysis and Literary Criticism" is essentially an examination of these dangers.

An even better example of "good" psychological interpretations is Stephen Logan's essay "The Soul of C. S. Lewis" published in *C. S. Lewis at Poets' Corner*.[99] I mention it because it is daring yet responsible, and it so well illustrates some of the things we have been talking about. Logan proposes a theory that cannot be evaluated on the present "historical data." It is that Lewis might have found his relationship with his mother "disappointing to him."[100] And that Lewis possibly remained unconscious of this. "Did he feel securely and lovingly held by his mother," Logan asks. "Was he welcomed into the world?"[101] These are terrific questions. How would one evaluate them? Even Logan, who is a professional psychiatrist, sends us to biography: "We would need to know a lot more about Flora Hamilton, and her feelings towards her son, in order to be able even to speculate with any confidence."[102]

Wiley-Blackwell, 2014), 7–29.

[98] Compare Medcalf's responsible carefulness with Prickett's assumption that a character flaw or vice, such as "consumerism," when "presented as through the eyes of a woman [is] perhaps illustrative of misogyny" (Prickett, "It Makes No Difference," 192). This weak presupposition leads Prickett to commit Personal Opinion Fallacies about Lewis's views on gender (for example, 191: "women being the natural location [for Lewis] of all that is trivial and worthless—recall the unexpected fate of Susan in the Narnia stories").

[99] Stephen Logan, "The Soul of C. S. Lewis," in *C. S. Lewis at Poets' Corner*, ed. by Michael Ward and Peter S. Williams (Eugene, OR: Cascade, 2016), 166–85.

[100] Logan, *Soul*, 179.

[101] Logan, *Soul*, 180.

[102] Logan, *Soul*, 180.

I will end with this. Tolkien exhibits a similar maturity. After his wife Edith's death, Tolkien wrote a beautiful letter to his son Christopher. Christopher had asked about the inscription Tolkien had chosen for Edith's tombstone: "Lúthien," the name of a central heroine in Tolkien's invented mythology. Tolkien explains: "[Your mother] was (and knew she was) my Lúthien. . . . I will say no more now. But I should like ere long to have a long talk with *you*. For if as seems probable I shall never write any ordered biography—it is against my nature, which expresses itself about things deepest felt in tales and myths—someone close in heart to me should know something about things that records do not record."[103] Tolkien's tales and myths are pregnant, so to speak, with "things deepest felt." But to safeguard real history, and to avoid future misunderstanding, he wants to . . . *talk* with his son, so that other, more personal, accounts might record what was imaginatively recorded in myth and tale.

---

[103] Letter of 11 July 1972, in J.R.R. Tolkien, *The Letters of J.R.R. Tolkien: A Selection*, ed. by Humphrey Carpenter (London: HarperCollins, 2006), 420–1.

C. S. Lewis and the Historical Imagination

JAMIN METCALF AND K. ALAN SNYDER

In 1925, the year that C. S. Lewis was first elected as a fellow and tutor at Magdalen College, Oxford, he went on a Spring holiday in the south of England. On this trip, Lewis took time to visit Salisbury Cathedral—one of the most magnificent examples of early gothic architecture in all of Europe. Though Lewis was still firmly ensconced in his atheism, he recognized a deep historical significance in this thirteenth-century Christian monument. As he noted in a letter to his father after the trip, Salisbury Cathedral was not only a beautiful piece of architecture, but a symbol of a bygone era which saw the world in a fundamentally different way than modern men. As Lewis put it:

> What impressed me most—the same thought has come into everyone's head in such places—was the force of Mind: the thousands of tons of masonry held in place by an idea, a religion: buttress, window, acres of carving, the very lifeblood of men's work, all piled up there and gloriously USELESS from the side of the base utility for which alone we build now. It really is typical of a change—the medieval town where the shops and houses huddle at the foot of the cathedral, and the modern city where the churches huddle between sky scraping offices and the appalling "stores."[1]

One of the interesting aspects of this off-hand reflection from Lewis is the imaginative way in which he thinks about this historical monument in

---

[1] Letter of April 1925, in C. S. Lewis, *The Collected Letters of C. S. Lewis*, ed. by Walter Hooper, 3 vols. (San Francisco: HarperCollins, 2004-7), 1: 639. Hereafter *CL*.

particular and of medieval history in general. It is indicative of a unique perspective that Lewis developed and maintained later in his work as a literary historian.

What role should the imagination play in historical inquiry? Much has been written about how Lewis's understanding of the imagination influenced both his literary and apologetic work. However, very little has been said about how his view of the imagination influenced his work as a literary historian. Throughout Lewis's career at both Oxford and Cambridge, he argued for a unique approach that privileged the role of the imagination both in the study and composition of history.

Lewis's writings indicate that he thought that historians and lay readers of history alike should cultivate what may here be called a *historical imagination*. This cultivation involved a careful attention to the use of language to convey historical ideas as well as a habitual willingness to see through the eyes of people from the past. In Lewis's own work as a literary historian, he exemplified this principle and concluded that it is through the imagination that history fulfills its primary purpose as a *liberal art*—an art that is conducive to human freedom and human flourishing. This distinct vision of history was grounded in the epistemological conclusions Lewis reached in his early life as a student of philosophy and was later reinforced by his conversion to Christianity. In order fully to understand and appreciate Lewis's vision, it is necessary to (1) reflect on Lewis's understanding of human imagination, (2) demonstrate how this understanding undergirded his work as a literary historian, and (3) describe the various implications of such an approach to historical study.

Imagination and Epistemology

Those who have studied Lewis's work on human imagination know all too well how difficult it is to pin down a precise definition of what he meant when he used the term. Much of this confusion comes from the ways in which Lewis's understanding of this concept changed throughout his life. In his autobiography, *Surprised by Joy*, he describes early experiences in his childhood of an illusory "desire" or "longing for the longing that had just ceased" while reading mythology, fairy stories, and romantic poetry.[2]

---

[2] C. S. Lewis, *Surprised by Joy: The Shape of My Early Life* (New York: HarperCollins, 2017), 18.

These experiences gave him a keen awareness of a phenomenon that he did not quite know how to articulate until "The Great War" with his friend Owen Barfield.³ This series of philosophical debates spurred Lewis to consider the subject of human imagination and aesthetic experience more thoroughly.

The principal conflict of "The Great War" was centered on whether or not imagination carried epistemological significance. In other words, can the imagination justly separate truth from falsehood? Did Lewis's experiences of "desire" while reading poetry reveal some truth or was it simply a pleasing aesthetic experience? Barfield argued for the affirmative in this debate, whereas Lewis (initially) held the negative view. What both men did agree on, however, was that the modern understanding of the imagination was reductionistic at best and woefully misguided at worst. Human imagination and aesthetic experience are not merely fanciful thoughts disconnected from reality. Rather, in their view, imagination is more deeply connected to the essential experiences of being human. Both Lewis and Barfield could see that the modern emphasis on empirical sciences and calculative reason had diminished the importance of the imagination, but they could not agree on what role the imagination should serve in our thinking. In a sense, both men agreed on the diagnosis but not the prognosis.⁴

In Barfield's book, *Poetic Diction*, he attempts to give a fuller philosophical defense of his thoughts on this very issue. At the heart of his defense is a careful analysis of how poets' use of metaphors and analogies produces a "felt change of consciousness" within their readers.⁵ Barfield argues that almost all language has metaphorical origins and that the recognition and absorption of metaphors gives human beings an expanded knowledge of the truth and meaning of things themselves. Though Lewis never fully accepted Barfield's conclusions, these arguments had a profound influence on his thought.

Interestingly, one of the first revelations that Owen Barfield gave Lewis on the topic of the imagination also influenced the way he thought about history itself. In *Surprised by Joy*, Lewis says, "Barfield . . . made short work

---

³ Lewis, *Surprised by Joy*, 242.

⁴ Stephen Thorson, *Joy and the Poetic Imagination* (Hamden, CT: Winged Lion Press, 2015), 12-15.

⁵ Owen Barfield, *Poetic Diction* (Middletown: Wesleyan University Press, 1973), 55.

of what I have called my 'chronological snobbery,' the uncritical acceptance of the intellectual climate common to our own age and the assumption that whatever has gone out of date is on that account discredited."[6] It was common in the intellectual climate of Lewis's day, as well as our own, to imagine that ideas that have gone out of date are disproved. But that is not always the case. The age of a thought says nothing at all about its truth or falsehood. "From seeing this," Lewis concluded, "one passes to the realization that our own age is also 'a period,' and certainly has, like all periods, its own characteristic illusions. They are likeliest to lurk in those widespread assumptions which are so ingrained in the age that no one dares to attack or feels it necessary to defend them."[7] This critique of "chronological snobbery" stayed with Lewis throughout his life and career—especially as a literary historian. It liberated Lewis from the false assumptions of his age by bringing attention to the ways in which one's imagination determines one's interpretation.

In the end, Lewis came around to the idea that the imagination did indeed have a role to play in epistemology—albeit a limited role with reason itself as the final arbiter. In his 1939 essay, "Bluspels and Flalansferes: A Semantic Nightmare," Lewis analyzes the ways in which dead metaphors, words and phrases that originally were metaphors but now are used as abstract terms in modern English, color our thought and language. Lewis uses Barfield's *Poetic Diction* as a starting point to address the question, "How far, if at all, is thinking limited by these dead metaphors?"[8] Lewis's answer is characteristically against the modern grain. He argues that whereas scientifically minded men of his day may claim that metaphorical language gets in the way of truth, the exact opposite is the case. He does this by pointing out the fact that much of what scientists call "literal" or "objective" language is actually full of forgotten metaphors.[9] Once this is remembered, the role of the imagination becomes essential. For reason cannot determine the truth or falsehood of any statement until the imagination determines its meaning. As Lewis puts it:

---

[6] Lewis, *Surprised by Joy*, 242.
[7] Lewis, *Surprised by Joy*, 243.
[8] C. S. Lewis, "Bluspels and Falansferes: A Semantic Nightmare," in *Selected Literary Essays*, ed. by Walter Hooper (Cambridge: Cambridge University Press, 2013), 252.
[9] Lewis, "Bluspels and Falansferes: A Semantic Nightmare," 264-5.

> It must not be supposed that I am in any sense putting forward the imagination as the organ of truth. We are not talking of truth, but of meaning: meaning which is the antecedent condition both of truth and falsehood, whose antithesis is not error but nonsense. I am a rationalist. For me, reason is the natural organ of truth; but imagination is the organ of meaning. Imagination, producing new metaphors or revivifying old, is not the cause of truth, but its condition. It is, I confess, undeniable that such a view indirectly implies a kind of truth or rightness in the imagination itself.[10]

Thus, for Lewis, though the imagination could not justify the truth of any assertion (Barfield's position), it was clear that it played a significant role in epistemology. It is the means by which we grasp meaning—the distinctive power that allows us to use our reason at all.

Lewis offers his most clear defense of what he saw as the imagination's role in epistemology in his famous essay, "Meditation in a Toolshed". In this essay, Lewis describes his experience of a beam of light pouring into a darkened shed. As Lewis looks at the beam and eventually steps into its light, he is able to distinguish two ways of experiencing, or knowing, the beam of light: (1) "looking at" the beam and (2) "looking along" it.[11] In *looking at* the beam, Lewis can see dust particles floating through it and discern the shape and direction of the beam itself. In *looking along* the beam, however, Lewis is able to see the world outside the shed: trees, birds, and the sun. What this image illustrates are two distinct ways of knowing. The first is, according to Lewis, "the whole basis of the specifically 'modern' type of thought."[12] It is the central mode of the scientific method, of data analysis, of objective observation, and of modern historical scholarship.

On the other hand, the second mode of knowing, that of "looking along," is the way of direct experience and of imagination. This is the mode of knowledge that Lewis believed was under attack in the modern world. As he put it, as soon as someone recognized these two modes of experience, a question arises:

---

[10] Lewis, "Bluspels and Falansferes: A Semantic Nightmare," 265.
[11] C. S. Lewis, "Meditation in a Toolshed," in *God in the Dock*, ed. by Walter Hooper (Grand Rapids: Eerdmans, 2014), 230.
[12] Lewis, "Meditation in a Toolshed," 232.

Which is the "true" or "valid" experience? Which tells you most about the thing? And you can hardly ask that question without noticing that for the last fifty years or so everyone has been taking the answer for granted. It has been assumed without discussion that if you want the true account of religion you must go, not to religious people, but to anthropologists; that if you want the true account of sexual love you must go, not to lovers, but to psychologists; that if you want to understand some "ideology" (such as medieval chivalry or the nineteenth-century idea of a "gentleman"), you must listen not to those who lived inside it, but to sociologists.[13]

As Lewis goes on to assert in the article, there is no rational basis for rejecting the experience of "looking along" in favor of "looking at." In fact, in many cases it is precisely the former that can yield true knowledge of a thing. In this instance, Lewis is clearly using this argument as a Christian apologist to defend the experiential knowledge of religion. However, the implications for other disciplines, such as history, are not hard to see. Scientists and historians alike "must, on pain of idiocy, deny from the very outset the idea that looking at is, by its own nature, intrinsically truer or better than looking along. One must look both along and at everything."[14]

Looking Along History

As Lewis notes in his autobiographical work, *Surprised by Joy*, G.K. Chesterton's work of historical apologetics, *The Everlasting Man*, exercised a profound influence on his development as a scholar.[15] In a section of Chesterton's work where he attempts to describe the ancient Greek and Roman transition from a mythological culture to a philosophical one, he makes a brief remark that seems to indicate the importance of the imagination in historical study. "The psychology of it," Chesterton says, "is really human enough to anyone who will try that experiment of seeing history from the inside."[16] This experiment of seeing "from the inside" seems to be very much in line with Lewis's metaphor of "seeing along"—of using the imagination to share in the experiences of others. Not surprisingly,

---

[13] Lewis, "Meditation in a Toolshed," 232.
[14] Lewis, "Meditation in a Toolshed," 232.
[15] Lewis, *Surprised by Joy*, 190-1.
[16] G. K. Chesterton, *The Everlasting Man* (Mineola, NY: Dover Publications, 2007), 155.

when one looks carefully at Lewis's historical writings, it becomes clear that this very experiment was at the heart of his work.

In 1927, Lewis wrote a letter to his brother, Warnie, in which he reflected on his recent study of Edward Gibbon's seminal book, *The History of the Decline and Fall of the Roman Empire*. "I am almost coming to the conclusion that all histories are bad," Lewis writes.[17] "Whenever one turns from the historian to the writings of the people he deals with there is always such a difference."[18] As Lewis goes on to explain, Gibbon, and other historians like him, write about historical events in such a way that, though factual, do little to communicate the significance and meaning that these events held for the actual people involved in them. Lewis compares Gibbon's account of Germanic warrior culture in the fifth century with those found in *Beowulf* and other medieval accounts of the same period:

> What a common measure is there between 'Odoacer had alienated the sympathies of his Italian subjects by seizing a third of the land to reward his veterans' and "Oft Scyld Scefing overthrew the mead benches of many kindred. The dwellers round had to obey him across the whales's way. That was a good king. . . . So shall a young hero *do good* and give lordly gifts, that his retainers may repay him when war comes" [*Beowulf*, 2. 4-24]. The implication (always present) in the first version that Odoacer oughtn't to have given the land to his men, or that any choice in the matter could have occurred to him, as against the perfectly untroubled sincerity with which the other describes the hero as "doing good" in scattering the "lordly gifts" (acquired no doubt at the cost of 'alienating the sympathy' of someone) makes one despair.[19]

What this comparison illustrates quite well is the important role that the imagination and language both play in the discipline of history. What Lewis is pointing out is that one can "see in some sense that the two passages refer to the same sort of fact. But what is left of the 'fact' if you take away both its two 'appearances'?"[20] In other words, Lewis can see that Gibbon lacked a historical imagination. He was able to correctly *look at* a historical event but had not sufficiently *looked along* it.

---

[17] Letter of 12 December 1927, in Lewis, *CL*, 1:174.
[18] Letter of 12 December 1927, in Lewis, *CL*, 1:174.
[19] Letter of 12 December 1927, in Lewis, *CL*, 1:174.
[20] Letter of 12 December 1927, in Lewis, *CL*, 1:174.

Lewis's critique of Gibbon is two-pronged in nature. On the one hand, Lewis is demonstrating how Gibbon's interpretation of Odoacer's actions is fundamentally conditioned by his modern outlook. On the other hand, Lewis is showing how language itself can give such vastly different senses of the same event. He does this by comparing Gibbon's words with those of the ninth-century poem, *Beowulf*, and the difference is dramatic. Gibbon gets the historical facts right, but his understanding of their significance—of their meaning—is questionable at best. This calls to mind Lewis's conclusions about the imagination in "Bluspels and Flalansferes: A Semantic Nightmare." In history, just as in other disciplines, the imagination serves as the "organ of meaning" and meaning "is the antecedent condition both of truth and falsehood."[21] Without the imagination and without attention to the way in which language engages the imagination, it is easy to fall into the same trap that Gibbon did.

So, how did Lewis avoid this trap in his own historical work? On the theoretical front, it seems that Lewis thought that disciplining his imagination to understand each historical era on its own terms was essential. In an essay aptly titled "De Audiendus Poetis," which roughly translates to "Listening to the Poets," Lewis wrote, "In so far as we are historians, there is no question. When our aim is knowledge we must go as far as all available means—including the most intense, yet at the same time most sternly disciplined, exercise of our imaginations—can possibly take us."[22] By "discipline," Lewis seems to mean that the historian must deliberately train his imagination to attend to the experience of those who lived the history itself. In other words, the historian must strive to gain "the experience of men long dead.... We must clean the lens and remove the stain so that the real past can be seen better."[23] Lewis compares this process to traveling in a foreign land. One may bring one's own culture into a foreign country as a tourist, or one can do all that he can to enjoy the country as an inhabitant might. The latter can transform and expand one's understanding, whereas the former leaves one unchanged.

There really is no great mystery as to how Lewis himself disciplined his imagination. In 1934, an American scholar, Sister Madeleva, wrote

---

[21] Lewis, "Bluspels and Falansferes: A Semantic Nightmare," 265.
[22] C. S. Lewis, "De Audiendus Poetis," in *Studies in Medieval and Renaissance Literature*, ed. by Walter Hooper (Cambridge: Cambridge University Press, 2013), 2.
[23] Lewis, "De Audiendus Poetis," 2.

to Lewis and asked him to describe his method for writing his famous "Prolegomena" lectures (which were later published in *The Discarded Image*). As Lewis explained:

> The process is inductive for the most part of my lecture: tho' on allegory, courtly love, and (sometimes) in philosophy, it is deductive —i.e. I *start* from the authors I quote. I elaborate this point because, if you are thinking of doing the same kind of thing (i.e. telling people what they ought to know as the *prius* of a study of medieval vernacular poets) I think you would be wise to work in the same way—starting *from* the texts you want to explain. You will soon find of course that you are working the other way at the same time, that you can correct current explanations, or see things to explain where the ordinary editors see nothing.[24]

By steeping himself in the literature of the era he was studying, Lewis not only collected facts but learned to see the world through the eyes of those bygone authors. He looked to primary sources first and allowed the experiences, attitudes, mores, and expressions found in them to shape his understanding of the past. As he said himself in his seminal work, *An Experiment in Criticism*, "My own eyes are not enough for me, I will see through the eyes of others. Reality, even seen through the eyes of many, is not enough. I will see what others have invented."[25]

The fruit of this discipline can be seen in Lewis's two most famous historical works: *The Discarded Image* and *English Literature in the Sixteenth Century*. The former is almost exclusively dedicated to helping students of medieval literature gain this disciplined imagination. The primary thesis of the book is that "in every period the Model of the Universe which is accepted by the great thinkers helps to provide what we may call a backcloth for the arts."[26] Lewis describes this "backcloth" upon which medieval literature was written in magnificent detail and in doing so, often takes time to head off modern assumptions that might get in the way of understanding medieval literature on its own terms.

For example, near the beginning of the book, Lewis sets out to

---

[24] Letter of 7 June 1934, in Lewis, *CL*, 2:141-2.

[25] C. S. Lewis, *An Experiment in Criticism* (Cambridge: Cambridge University Press, 2013), 140.

[26] C. S. Lewis, *The Discarded Image* (Cambridge: Cambridge University Press, 2013), 14.

correct the all-too-common assumption that medieval beliefs about the supernatural were a sign of their savageness. On the contrary, as Lewis points out, "the English poet knew nothing about that. . . . He believes in these daemons because he has read about them in a book; just as most of us believe in the Solar System or in the anthropologists' accounts of early man."[27] In this short passage, Lewis draws the reader's attention to the contingencies surrounding the medieval worldview, while also pointing out the contingencies of his own. This double-edged effect is a common trope in Lewis's historical work and is very much the result of his imaginative approach to history.

In a similar fashion, Lewis describes how "Medieval historians dealt hardly at all with the impersonal. Social or economic conditions and national characteristics come in only by accident or when they are required to explain something in the narrative."[28] Lewis puts this tendency of medieval authors in tension with the modern propensity to use impersonal forces and '-isms' to explain historical events. As Lewis half-jokingly observes, "Perhaps past or future ages might wonder at the predominance of the impersonal in some modern histories; might even ask, 'But were there no *people* at that time?'"[29] What Lewis is doing here is training his readers to use their imagination to attend to the context of medieval authors, while also drawing their attention to the literary nature of history itself. "Historians," Lewis goes on to explain, "even in dealing with contemporary events, will pick out those elements which the habitual bent of their imagination has conditioned them to notice."[30] Lewis does not say that their *reason* has conditioned them, but rather that their *imagination* has conditioned them. This is wholly consistent with his understanding of the human imagination and the essential role that it plays in the discipline of history.

Lewis devotes several pages of *The Discarded Image* to a detailed explanation of one book from the medieval period: Boethius's *De Consolatione Philosophiae*. Lewis does so because this one work of philosophical inquiry was so influential on medieval thought that "to acquire a taste for it is almost

---

[27] Lewis, *The Discarded Image*, 2-3.
[28] Lewis, *The Discarded Image*, 182.
[29] Lewis, *The Discarded Image*, 182.
[30] Lewis, *The Discarded Image*, 182.

to become naturalized in the Middle Ages."[31] For example, in Book II of the Consolation, Boethius offers an apologia for *Fortuna*—a personified picture of fortune, or the forces that determine human wellbeing and failure. In these passages, Boethius offers "one of the most vigorous defenses against the view . . . which 'comforts cruel men' by interpreting variations of human prosperity as divine rewards or punishments."[32] As Lewis goes on to explain, this argument was hugely influential on the culture, art, philosophy, and people's understanding of history in the Middle Ages. It taught them not to interpret historical outcomes as moral judgments. It also stands as a foil to many modern philosophies of history, such as "the Whig interpretation of history' and . . . the philosophy of Carlyle."[33] The Whig interpretation is an approach to historiography that presents history as a journey from an oppressive and benighted past to a "glorious present," and Thomas Carlyle was a nineteenth century philosopher who postulated what is now known as the "Great Man Theory" of history, which contends that human history progresses through the influence of exceptional individuals. Both of these philosophies dismiss the warnings of Boethius.

By studying Boethius, Lewis was able simultaneously to demonstrate how medieval interpretations of history were conditioned by the imagination and how modern interpretations of history have been conditioned by the imagination. The tendency to interpret historical outcomes as moral judgments is endemic in modern philosophies of history, such as Marxism and Hegelianism, which interpret human history as a progressive movement toward liberation. Both of these schools of thought draw conclusions from history that go beyond the scope of true historical inquiry. In Lewis's essay, "Historicism," he makes a clear distinction between historians and historicists. The former use imagination in their writings in an acceptable way; the latter, though, tend to allow imagination to take an unearned preeminence. What he means by this is that the historicist always looks for an "inner meaning" in history. He believes that "events fell out as they did because of some ultimate, transcendent necessity in the ground of things."[34]

---

[31] Lewis, *The Discarded Image*, 75.
[32] Lewis, *The Discarded Image*, 82.
[33] Lewis, *The Discarded Image*, 82.
[34] C. S. Lewis, "Historicism," in *The Seeing Eye* (New York: Ballantine Books, 1967), 131.

The historicist also believes that the future can be predicted since he knows the inner meaning of the historical process. This differs from the genuine historian. "A historian, without becoming a Historicist, may certainly infer unknown events from known ones. He may even infer future events from past ones; prediction may be a folly, but it is not Historicism."[35] Furthermore, he sees nothing inimical to the historical profession when one tries to interpret history by attempting to imaginatively place oneself in the position of a person living in an earlier era. Making the past more real is an understandable and acceptable goal for historians. In fact, it is precisely this method of historical inquiry that gives one the ability to see the flaws in historicism, as Lewis demonstrates in *The Discarded Image*.

Lewis does similar historical work in *English Literature in the Sixteenth Century*. At the outset of the book, Lewis says that his primary aim is "to sketch some of the intellectual and imaginative conditions under which [Elizabethan authors] wrote."[36] As he proceeds with this work, he attempts to prune modern assumptions in order to orient his readers' imaginations for the task. For example, in a section discussing the changing cosmologies of the sixteenth century, Lewis argues that "the literary historian . . . must even try to forget his knowledge of what comes after, and see the egg as if he did not know it was going to become a bird."[37] A failure to do so, Lewis warns, will impose a modern dichotomy on the men of that age and distort the real significance that the shifting notions of cosmology at that time had on them.

Lewis treats the religious violence of the sixteenth century with a similar cautiousness. He warns against heedlessly imposing anachronistic notions on the men of the sixteenth century. Again, Lewis contrasts modern assumptions with those of past in order to accomplish this:

> A modern, ordered to profess or recant a religious belief under pain of death, knows that he is being tempted and that the government which so tempts him is a government of villains. But this background was lacking when the period of religious revolution began. No man claimed for himself or allowed to another the right of believing as he

---

[35] Lewis, "Historicism," 131.
[36] C. S. Lewis, *English Literature in the Sixteenth Century: Excluding Drama* (Oxford: Oxford University Press, 1973), 2.
[37] Lewis, *English Literature in the Sixteenth Century*, 5.

chose. All parties inherited from the Middle Ages the assumption that Christian man could live only in a theocratic polity which had both the right and the duty of enforcing true religion by persecution. Those who resisted its authority did so not because they thought it had no right to impose doctrines but because they thought it was imposing the wrong ones.[38]

Again, Lewis invites his readers to not just *look at* the experiences of past people, but to *look along* their experiences—to train their imagination to see history from *the inside*, and in so doing gain a fuller and more accurate understanding of it. Accomplishing this, Lewis seemed to believe, not only gave readers a better understanding of historical eras but also allowed them to experience history as a truly liberal, and liberating, art.

History as a Liberal Art

As Lewis knew very well, higher education in the Middle Ages was not primarily focused on vocational training but on the liberal arts.[39] A liberal arts education, traditionally understood, means an education designed to form a free and virtuous person. Through studying a wide array of arts for their own sake, students learned not only how to succeed in a particular vocation, but how to think and live well. This view of education stands in contrast to more modern notions that prioritize the utilitarian, or practical, aspects of education. In studying Lewis's work in history, it is clear that he thought history, when studied in the imaginative mode previously mentioned, is a liberal art in the truest sense of the term. Two very important implications can be drawn from this view. The first is that history, imaginatively understood, has a liberating effect on one's mind. The second is that developing a historical imagination is something that all students, not just historians, should learn to do.

In *A Preface to Paradise Lost*, Lewis quotes G. K. Chesterton as he attempts to help his readers understand the significance and meaning behind Milton's great English epic. "Any man who is cut off from the past," Lewis quotes, "is a man most unjustly disinherited."[40] This is a uniquely

---

[38] Lewis, *English Literature in the Sixteenth Century*, 39.
[39] Lewis, *The Discarded Image*, 187.
[40] G. K. Chesterton, "On Man: The Heir of All Ages," in *Avowals and Denials* (London: Methuen, 1934) 83.

high view of history. Far from viewing history as a catalogue for practical use, or an interest to be pursued by a few bookish scholars, both Chesterton and Lewis lift it to the level of "inheritance"—of a gift to be received and bestowed by all. Using several quotations from Chesterton's "On Man: The Heir of All Ages," Lewis goes on to explain:

> To enjoy our full humanity we ought, so far as is possible, to contain within us potentially at all times, and on occasions to actualize, all the modes of feeling and thinking through which man has passed. You must, so far as in you lies, become an Achaean chief while reading Homer, a medieval knight while reading Malory, and an eighteenth century Londoner while reading Johnson. Only thus will you be able to judge the work "in the same spirit that its author writ" and to avoid chimerical criticism.[41]

What becomes quite clear in this passage is the heavy emphasis Lewis places on the imaginative nature of history. For Lewis, the inheritance of history is not merely a collection of facts or dates but a kaleidoscope of worldviews that can enrich our lives and give us greater wisdom. This is a view that, as Lewis bemoans, has fallen out of fashion in modern education.

In Lewis's essay, "Modern Man and His Categories of Thoughts," he describes the consequences of modern education's shift away from the liberal arts and toward vocational training. "Education" Lewis argues, "was formerly based throughout Europe, on the Ancients."[42] This meant that men generally were trained to "believe that valuable truth could still be found in an ancient book. It was natural to them to reverence tradition. Values quite different from those of modern industrial civilization were constantly present to their minds."[43] The main consequence of losing this type of education "has been to isolate the mind in its own age; to give it, in relation to time, that disease which, in relation to space, we call Provincialism."[44] This *historical provincialism* is precisely what Lewis's work in history sought to combat. By engaging the imagination and seeing through the eyes of people from past ages, the student of imaginative history is liberated

---

[41] C. S. Lewis, *A Preface to Paradise Lost* (New York: HarperCollins, 2022), 64.
[42] C. S. Lewis, "Modern Man and His Categories of Thought," in *Present Concerns*, ed. by Walter Hooper (New York: HarperCollins, 2017) 62.
[43] Lewis, "Modern Man and His Categories of Thought," 62.
[44] Lewis, "Modern Man and His Categories of Thought," 62.

from a narrow set of assumptions particular to his or her historical era.

How exactly can an imaginative approach to history liberate one's mind? Lewis's argument, which he made in one form or another in several different works throughout his career, runs as follows. All people reason within the imaginative parameters of the culture they grew up in, and people in modern culture are no exception. This means that if one seeks the truth, it is vital that he expand his imaginative framework and consider the viewpoints of those who grew up in epochs vastly different from his own. One of the most effective ways that people can do this is by studying primary sources in an imaginative way; that is, by acquainting themselves with the imaginative frameworks of past ages through their writings and art. The more that one cultivates this historical imagination, the more perspective and imaginative space one gains to assess the accepted truths of one's own age.

Perhaps one of the most telling examples of this argument was articulated by Lewis in his inaugural lecture as the Chair of Medieval and Renaissance Literature at Cambridge University in 1954. In the lecture, Lewis warns that in individual lives and in society as a whole, "it is the forgotten past that enslaves us."[45] The only remedy, Lewis goes on to say, is an intimate and imaginative knowledge of history. As he argues, "to study the past does indeed liberate us from the present, from the idols of our own market-place. But I think it liberates us from the past too. I think no class of men are less enslaved to the past than historians" for the "unhistorical are usually, without knowing it, enslaved to a fairly recent past."[46] In other words, all people think and live within some imaginative framework or tradition. It cannot be escaped. The only option left to us is to decide how deep of a framework or tradition we choose to think and live within.

This same argument comes up in several other works by Lewis. In his essay, "On The Reading of Old Books," he points out that "every age has its own outlook. It is specially good at seeing certain truths and specially liable to make certain mistakes. We all, therefore, need the books that will correct the characteristic mistakes of our own period. And that means the

---

[45] C. S. Lewis, "*De Descriptione Temporum*," in *Selected Literary Essays*, ed. by Walter Hooper (Cambridge: Cambridge University Press, 2013), 12.

[46] Lewis, "*De Descriptione Temporum*," 12.

old books."[47] In another essay, "Is English Doomed?" he again argues that the main purpose of literary studies, including history, "is to lift the student out of his provincialism by making him 'the spectator,' if not of all, yet of much, 'time and existence' . . . to meet the past where alone the past still lives, [to be] taken out of the narrowness of his own age and class into a more public world."[48] In a sermon Lewis gave in 1939, "Learning in War-time," he again makes the same claim—this time with even more serious concern:

Most of all, perhaps, we need intimate knowledge of the past . . . to remind us that the basic assumptions have been quite different in different periods and that much which seems certain to the uneducated is merely temporary fashion. A man who has lived in many places is not likely to be deceived by the local errors of his native village; the scholar has lived in many times and is therefore in some degree immune from the great cataract of nonsense that pours from the press and the microphone of his own age.[49]

Lewis's phrase "intimate knowledge of the past" seems to indicate a deep sense of knowledge that goes beyond the realm of reason itself. This intimate knowledge can only be reached by way of a "most sternly disciplined exercise of our imaginations."[50] The result, as Lewis says, is a liberation of the mind. It gives the mind an immunity from the narrowness and blindness of the present age.

Conclusion

What role, then, does the imagination play in historical inquiry? According to C. S. Lewis, the imagination is nothing less than foundational. By cultivating a historical imagination, students of history can come not only to *look at* the facts of history but *look along* them—to see history from the inside and, in so doing, gain a deeper wisdom, insight, and enjoyment

---

[47] C. S. Lewis, "On the Reading of Old Books," in *God in the Dock*, ed. by Walter Hooper (Grand Rapids: Eerdmans, 2014), 219.

[48] C. S. Lewis, "Is English Doomed?" in *Present Concerns*, ed. by Walter Hooper (New York: HarperCollins, 2017) 29.

[49] C. S. Lewis, "Learning in War-Time" in *The Weight of Glory,* ed. by Walter Hooper (New York: HarperCollins, 2000) 58-59.

[50] Lewis, "De Audiendus Poetis," 2.

of it. As Lewis himself said, "being human, I am inquisitive, I want to know as well as to enjoy," and through the imaginative study of history "I should hope to be led by it to newer and fresher enjoyments, things I could never have met in my own period, modes of feeling, flavours, atmospheres, nowhere accessible but by a mental journey into the real past."[51] History is the just inheritance of mankind, and studying and teaching it in the same manner as C. S. Lewis may open up the opportunity to receive this inheritance as it was always meant to be.[52]

---

[51] Lewis, "De Audiendus Poetis," 4.

[52] Dr. K. Alan Snyder was awarded the 2022 Clyde Kilby Research Grant by the Marion E. Wade Center at Wheaton College for his research into Lewis's views on history.

Poetry

COMPILED BY BROOKS LAMPE

Under a Bridge Downtown

CHRIS JENSEN

I saw a man encircled by stuff: bottles, crates,
oven racks, the rusted hub of a wheel. In his hands
a pair of wooden drumsticks flashed with reckless precision
as he drubbed the tubs, rang the glass, and splashed the racks
into brilliant threads of sound like an ecstatic flag
that waved against the roar of cars overhead.

Some walked past and offered nods of admiration,
others dropped coins or bills, but whatever the cost
to him or to us he kept on hammering those cast-off pieces,
kept on making that truthful music, kept on plowing
that forlorn ground into a field of sound
until his wordless song grew like some mystical seed
thrown beside the road

and I could almost hear him say, take up
your own broken bits and do likewise.

When Dreams Die

Chris Jensen

I wonder in the whole history of the church
if a man ever brought a red-tailed hawk,
and one wounded, to Divine Liturgy?

He saw her that morning by the edge of the highway
lurching in circles over gravel and glass,
lured by the bait of road-kill squirrel
like some ironic Icarus who flew too low
into an ocean of asphalt
only to be struck by a speeding car while her mate
cried songs of concern from a nearby tree.

When our Samaritan pulled to the shoulder
he approached, spoke to it, made good plans.
Minutes later he came into the nave
cradling the wounded creature across his chest,
standing up front by the tall cross
while children softly approached, serious and calm,
like visiting a friend at the hospital. And they petted it.

Of course, we all hoped the mission of mercy
would end happily with a brief stay at the Audubon
and then a glorious release
but instead, right at noon, as the chanting ended
and the priests divested, the light slowly dimmed
in her wild eyes like two tiny coals gone cold.

No, the brave bird would never rise to fly
or find her branch of olive, instead spending her last hour
in the arms of the creature that paved her doom—
just another wounded soul in a world where death
must find its prey.

> Chris Jensen has taught English at Portland Community College
> for twenty-three years and is a deacon at the Eastern Orthodox Church
> of the Annunciation in Milwaukie, Oregon.

The Verge

J. Aleksandr Wootton

"But do you really mean, Sir," said Peter, "that there could be other worlds—all over the place, just round the corner—like that?" "Nothing is more probable," said the Professor.

—C.S. Lewis, *The Lion, The Witch, and the Wardrobe*

I have sentried the verge
of numinous worlds innumerable
up to brink brought meat and drink
for they are closer, more beautiful and
more perilous, and much closer
than we think.

They border our backyards,
brush against our bookshelves,
they chime out chary answer
to our brazen churchbells.

And should we at the thresholds
find us there with dusty key
or broken spine or florid leaf
or signal star, and if

our inner moths can no more resist
these otherworldly lights, give
your Atlas leave, for he never
held broad horizon up to brim
of all that, ever becoming, is.

J. Aleksandr Wootton is the pen name of Jason Smith, author of the much-loved YA fantasy series *Fayborn* and the poetry collection *Muninn Wandering*. His latest book is *28 Days to Save the World: Crafting Your Culture to be Ready for Anything* (co-authored with CEO Dan Purvis), an account of the massive ventilator manufacturing scale-up undertaken as part of U.S. pandemic response, coupled with a case study and how-to guide on designing and implementing an organization›s culture to thrive despite extraordinary challenge. Smith serves as a strategic advisor to the C.S. Lewis Foundation, on the board of An Unexpected Journal, and as the director of marketing and communication for the medical device engineering firm Velentium.

Reviews

Book Reviews

Jason M. Baxter, *The Medieval Mind of C. S. Lewis: How Great Books Shaped a Great Mind* (Downers Grove, IL: InterVarsity Press, 2022). 166 pages. $22.00. ISBN 9781514001646.

One of this book's aims is to advance Lewis's reputation as a professional academic and a literary scholar, specifically a medieval one, onto a more equal footing with his reputation as a Christian apologist and fiction writer. Throughout the Introduction, the author is at pains to justify this Lewis who writes about what "many of [his] readers" or the book's presumed audience (American evangelicals?) might describe as knowledge in "old, dusty books" and to persuade them that it is not "absurd, maybe even irresponsible and escapist, to the devote the whole of one's adult life to th[is] study" (5-6). There is a possible justification in tailoring a book on Lewis's medieval erudition to such a group (perhaps InterVarsity Press insisted on the deferential approach); after all, Lewis described himself—apologetically, though with tongue in cheek—as a living "dinosaur" (a specimen helpful to understanding the remote past) to his own generation—and in an academic setting no less. Nevertheless, one sympathizes with John Fleming's statement quoted from *The Cambridge Companion to C. S. Lewis*: "The professional medievalist must be somewhat bemused by the fact that the literary scholarship and criticism of C. S. Lewis is so little known among his general readership and to some not known at all. After all, teaching literature was Lewis's 'day job,' and he expended much energy and talent in writing about it" (5, n15).

The main chapters follow a somewhat consistent pattern of explicating a medieval author, book, or set of ideas and illustrating how Lewis used them in his own works. Chapter one introduces the medieval model of the universe (expounded in Lewis's *The Discarded Image*), principally based on

Cicero's "Dream of Scipio" as commented on by Macrobius, Calcidius's *On Plato's Timaeus*, and Boethius's *De Musicia*. Baxter focuses on the music of the spheres motif of these works and sees it operating in the creation scene of *The Magician's Nephew*, in which Aslan sings the universe into existence, and in the visit of the planetary intelligences to Ransom and Merlin in *That Hideous Strength*. "The important thing to note in these two passages, is that Lewis . . . set himself to re-create the medieval *harmonia mundi* of Macrobius, Boethius, and Calcidius" (32).

Chapter two touts Lewis's ability as a writer to create such compelling atmospheres of time and place that his readers can feel what it was like to visit a planet like Perelandra or a world like Narnia. Whether this talent derives from Lewis's medieval learning or is owed to the power of his own imagination is not differentiated, but Baxter claims that the medieval practice of *imitatio* in art is relevant and so echoes of Dante in *Perelandra* demonstrate Lewis's "craft as a writer" (49-50).

Chapter three describes Lewis's "medieval mind" in terms of his criticism of the modern world's hustle and bustle and mechanistic world view. He is a "new Boethius," critical of "the maladies of the new barbarians," i.e., modern humanity (59). *English Literature of the Sixteenth Century* and *The Abolition of Man* represent two of the clearest discussions of this criticism, which includes resistance to "disenchanting the universe . . . and casting doubt on the very possibility of rationality" (64).

Chapter four discusses how habits of verbal expression subconsciously convey a "cosmology" or "world picture": in particular, the "linguistic world we live in is peculiarly ill-suited to spiritual desire," preventing moderns from imagining an alternative to naturalism or a "mechanized world picture" (72-73). This "evil enchantment" is illustrated in *The Silver Chair* by the lower-world Witch's denial of the existence of Narnia above ground (74-75) and *The Abolition of Man*, which describes modern education as inculcating a Gradgrindian rule of facts and a rejection of "just sentiments," i.e., values: "modern education divorces the heart and mind" (81). Hugh of St. Victor and Thomas Traherne are quoted for their high appraisal of creation and nature, which counterposes a mechanistic perspective, and Lewis's essay "The Necessity of Chivalry" for its promotion of values like courage, civility, and gentleness.

Chapter five focuses on how Lewis admired Dante's literary modeling of "speak[ing] of spiritual realities in a way in which they felt real, attractive, and weighty" (87). "Dante taught him how an artist could cast a 'counterspell' in which the good feels weighty and attractive, a spell to overcome the 'evil enchantment' cast by modernity" (88). Lewis's work indebted to Dante that best reflects this quality is *The Great Divorce*, in which, to a hellish ghost, a blade of grass is diamond-hard and a flower is heavier than a boulder in the substantive reality of heaven.

Chapter six examines "the presence of mystical theology in Lewis's life" (104). *The Cloud of Unknowing* was one of his favorite medieval works, and Rudolph Otto's *The Idea of the Holy* one of the books that most influenced his faith. Otto's theme is the numinous, and "the concept of the numinous is absolutely everywhere in Lewis's writings" (109). The most developed episode that illustrates this concept is Lucy's deep-night, mystical encounter with Aslan in *Prince Caspian*: "in this scene, perhaps more completely than any other in Lewis's imaginative writings, we find the medievalist bringing together all the varied melodic strands of his thoughts on mysticism. It is a blend of the terrible, the awful, the profound, and the transcendent; but also . . . the homely, the personal, the lovingly intimate" (118).

Chapter seven discusses the medieval concept of *praeparatio evangelica*, which refers to how "non-Christian cultures . . . played a crucial role in preparing the world for the gospel of Christ" (122). Dante's Statius and Virgil's "Fourth Eclogue" are two such touchstones. Baxter believes Lewis was personally committed to this concept since his own conversion story follows this pattern: "the idea of *praeparatio evangelica* is not just at the heart of Lewis's own conversion but also at the heart of his 'philosophy of religion'"; "it was important for him to be able to explain what was true about non-Christian religions" (125). As Lewis states in "Religion Without Dogma?" "my conversion, very largely, depended on recognizing Christianity as the completion, the actualization, the entelechy, of something that had never been fully absent from the mind of man" (125). This topic applies to Lewis's life and theology but not, in Baxter's explication, his imaginative works. The chapter shifts to a treatment of "deep conversion," which is exemplified at the end of Dante's *Purgatorio* and imitated by Lewis in passages from *The Great Divorce* and Orual's repentance scene and urged as the process of "unveiling," i.e., "letting ourselves become known to God" (which Lewis admired so much as the point of Buber's *I and Thou*) in *Letters to Malcolm* (139).

As expounded primarily in the Epilogue of *The Discarded Image*, chapter eight reveals why, in Lewis's mind, modern science does not undermine a medieval "mythical" or "metaphorical" world view. First, medieval cosmology as a symbolic structure does not claim to be pure fact; second, modern science also depends on metaphorical estimations and constructs to model its theoretical conception of the universe. Hence, one can even speak of "how modern science and ancient mythology could be reconciled" (144): "For both medievals and moderns, mysterious entities, hardly understood, emerge out of darkness. . . . For modern cosmologists . . . the universe is packed full of marvels and strange entities" (156). By recognizing that "modern cosmology . . . can be seen in a religious and poetic sense" (156), Lewis was free to reuse medieval notions of the universe and invent space fiction and Narnian worlds in which theological dramas play out.

The Conclusion puts in context how Lewis, Tolkien, and other champions of the remote past found its "exuberant joy" an antidote, not just to secular unbelief, but also to a theism shorn of the supernatural and lacking the vitality of pagan religion. For Lewis, modernist faith exhibits a "dolorous piety" and is a "minimal religion" that has "nothing that can convince, convert, or . . . console: nothing, therefore, which can restore vitality to our civilization. It [modern belief] is not costly enough" (160, quoting from "Religion without Dogma?"). Their "nostalgia" for antiquity or "older" ages was really a yearning for "Other Time," which would allow these writers to "stand outside [their] own time, outside Time itself, maybe" (160). The premoderns "peopled air and earth and water with gods and goddesses, nymphs and elves" (163), an inspirited world from which we moderns feel cut off, exiled. But this alienation can be an "extraordinary stimulus to hope" (162). This hope found its incarnation in the imagination of C. S. Lewis and his attention to "the old model" that embodied a "deep, human subconscious desire for a world . . . we are meant to occupy, but not yet" (164).

The book's title and focus seem to privilege viewing Lewis as first and foremost a medievalist in his learning and writings. Certainly, he was a great medieval scholar, but his own chronology for the life of "Old Western Man" extends well into the nineteenth century. It seems a little reductive to link his accomplishments to the study of the Middle Ages alone. He was also a great classicist, a great critic of sixteenth- and seventeenth-century literature, viewed himself as an advocate of Romanticism, and was learned in classical and modern philosophy. Medieval traditions such as direct borrowings and literary imitation can be found in the modernist poems *The Wasteland* and *The Four Quartets*, and the ability to create tangible descriptions of the next world owes as much to Plato's thought as to Dante: for example, in the penultimate scene of *The Last Battle*, while the chief characters race "further up and further in," Lord Digory exclaims, "It's all in Plato, all in Plato!" (chapter fifteen).

In addition to the analyses of direct correspondences drawn between certain medieval authors, ideas, and literary devices and Lewis's own work, Jason Baxter's book should be recognized for its richer, deeper, more expansive treatment of additional medieval topics in each chapter than are mentioned in the summaries above. For example, there are extended discussions of significant topics, such as time as an image of eternity, *lectio divina*, Boethius on reason and imagination, Abbot Suger on the material excess of Notre Dame cathedral and its evocation of spiritual meanings, and much else. As a scholar of the Middle Ages himself, Professor Baxter is an excellent guide to Lewis's medieval learning and his use of it in his fiction and apologetics.

WILLIAM GENTRUP
Arizona State University

P. H. Brazier, *A Hebraic Inkling: C. S. Lewis on Judaism and the Jews* (Eugene, OR, Pickwick Publications, 2021). 301 pages. $34.99. ISBN 9781725291973

The author's stated purpose in *A Hebraic Inkling* is to demonstrate the development of Lewis's thought, from dismissing to esteeming the Hebraic mindset. "Hebraic" in the title of this book is specifically defined by the author as "relating to the Jewish people, especially the Hebrews of ancient Israel, and to Judaism, the religion of the chosen people of God" (xvii). It will help the reader to keep this in mind as the author weaves and skips between various sub-topics that fit under the umbrella of this term.

Brazier's endeavor is a difficult prospect, as there is relatively little material until after Lewis's conversion. Consequently, with the exception of one letter,[1] Brazier uses generalizations about the era to demonstrate his case. When Lewis's conversion is referenced, Brazier introduces Hebraic ontology. However, he spends little time developing this line of thought, so that the conclusion seems forced. This pattern is repeated as the book winds through various topics, unsatisfactorily concluding one, before shifting focus to another that may seem tangential. For one example, Brazier is insightful when discussing the Hebrew names of God, and how the revealing of the names mirrors the "evolving conversion" (60) of Lewis's Christian walk. It would have been interesting to have this expanded upon, but the chapter ends abruptly.

Also problematic is the uneven tone of the book. Sometimes it is scholarly, sometimes obscure, and to some degree, confrontational. The book is sprinkled with sharp remarks towards those who hold to ideologies the author disagrees with. While they may have been intended as ironic humor, they play more like quick jabs, and lack a sense of humility that would give them consideration. Throughout the book, phrases by the author or quotes of Lewis are repeated but provide no additional weight to the line of reasoning by this repetition.

When Brazier moves to the section on scripture, primarily the Psalms, there is ample material to work with. He analyzes the structure of Hebrew poetry, highlighting the parallelism and the ability to survive translation, which Lewis had observed. The author surveys topics of creation, judgment, and prefigurement within the Psalms. While he integrates Lewis's views on prefigurement with his own, readers may be surprised at Brazier's challenge of Lewis over the imprecatory Psalm 137. He critically observes, "Lewis almost automatically objects to the infanticide called for" (122) and defends the psalmist as "at least candid, truthful and authentic" (124).

The author is not an apologist, yet Brazier writes from the perspective of one who believes both the Hebrew and Christian (Old and New Testament) scriptures, as C. S. Lewis did. In fact, he also assumes his

---

[1] Letter of 20 April 1921 in C. S. Lewis, *The Collected Letters of C. S. Lewis*, ed. by Walter Hooper, 3 vols. (San Francisco: HarperCollins, 2004-7), 1:536-8.

audience is Christian when describing Christ and related doctrine. Despite the ostensible thesis of *A Hebraic Inkling*, another theme is at work. Throughout the book, Brazier argues for the re-evaluation of Western church conceptions to embrace the Jewishness of Jesus. To emphasize this, he frequently uses the word *Yeshua* in place of *Jesus* to provide more emphasis on the Jewishness of the Messiah. He states that translating the word from Hebrew "into Greek and Latin–*Christos*, the Christ–it takes on a different, possibly, more universal character," (179) although he does maintain that this character is rooted in the Hebrew notion. One passage that Brazier omits concerns Lewis's own words from *Surprised by Joy*: "I was in that state of mind in which a boy thinks it extremely telling to call God Jahweh, and Jesus, Jeshua."[2] The younger Lewis may have had an ally in Brazier.

Some reflections of the author do not derive from Lewis, such as "Christianity is to be seen as an extension of Judaism" (76), and "the nature of the Torah, which is still considered valid and relevant, and is thus binding on those of faith in Yeshua" (196). These and other passages extend the author's gaze beyond Lewis and edge close to advocating the primacy of Hebraic as *opposed* to "Christian" thinking.

His third section titled "Family" uses Lewis's theological development to extend Brazier's own understanding of the Messianic Jew and the chosen status of the nation. In the last chapter on family life with Joy and her sons, Brazier inclines more towards admiration than assessment. He extols Joy for her insight as a converted Jew but fails to balance this portrayal with the discernment revealed in Santamaria's exceptional biography, *Joy: Poet, Seeker, and the Woman who Captivated C. S. Lewis*.[3] The final pages on Douglas and David Gresham lean more towards family bickering (however righteous) than academic inquiry; it leaves a dismal reverberation as the section ends.

The book contains the usual barbarisms and errors that are common in current publishing. Some run-on sentences could benefit from editing. Those with an appreciation for the Hebrew Scriptures and current Messianic thought will find the book familiar. For those interested in the intersection

---

[2] C. S. Lewis, *Surprised by Joy* (New York: Harcourt Brace, 1995), 173.
[3] Abigail Santamaria, *Joy: Poet, Seeker, and the Woman who Captivated C. S. Lewis* (London: SPCK, 2015).

of Hebraic and Lewis studies, it could serve as an index for researching the letters and other writings by Lewis. Although *Hebraic Inkling* proffers an interesting delve into Lewisiana, the result is less than the sum of its parts. One Lewis aphorism that Brazier uses to good effect is "all that was best in Judaism survives in Christianity."[4] It gives a valid pause to reflect on the current perspective of the church towards its Hebraic roots. One is left wondering if the author would invert the saying to "all that is best in Christianity is met eschatologically in Judaism." However, the case has not been substantiated from Lewis's own reflections on the Scriptures.

ERIN SEIDEL
Ridgefield, Washington

James Como, *Mystical Perelandra: My Lifelong Reading of C. S. Lewis and His Favorite Book* (Hamden, CT: Winged Lion Press, 2022). 148 pages. $16.99. ISBN 9781935688297.

James Como's recent release, *Mystical Perelandra*, is a bit of a departure from his previous publications. Como's text is a blend of memoir and critical analysis of a book that he calls a "revelation." In fact, it features excerpts of his other writings assembled and combined with new material in one volume. Following in the publication trend of other works such as Katharine Smyth's *All the Lives We've Ever Lived: Seeking Solace in Virginia Woolf*, James Como unpacks the literary impact of *Perelandra* and how that specific book, along with others in C. S. Lewis's corpus, changed Como's life.

Como writes that *Mystical Perelandra* was conceived "as a conversation intended to invite impressions, arguments, recollections, and opinions of fellow sojourners" (5). This book particularly argues that not only was Lewis a mystic, but *Perelandra* is "his fully formed Vision" (9). Como separates his treatise into six chapters: "The Tongue is Also a Fire," "Hope," "Storytelling," "Myth," "Strife," and "Awe." Como also includes

---

[4] C. S. Lewis, "Religion without Dogma," in *Undeceptions:Essays on Theology and Ethics*, ed. by Walter Hooper (London: Bles, 1971), 99-144.

a Bibliography, an inventory of Spiritual Writers, and Other Books of Interest. Essentially this book is a love letter to the works of C. S. Lewis and serves to illustrate how writing can ultimately alter our lives for the better.

One fascinating aspect (among many) of Como's text is his exploration of the spiritual journey of Ransom as parallel to his own. Como recalls fondly his first meeting of the New York C. S. Lewis Society, his first pilgrimage to Oxford, and initial meeting with Lewis's secretary Walter Hooper. Como's and Lewis's spiritual journeys share many resemblances. Similar to Lewis, Como lost his mother at a young age, a loss that left Como, his older brother, and his father inconsolable. Como writes, in a passage that echoes chapters from *Surprised by Joy*, that "the world shrank, my church-going became formulaic, my praying virtually ceased. For reasons that have no place in these reflections I was frightened, lonely, and isolated" (64). Como admits that two significant changes in his life occurred to sober him "out of the funk": finding the works of C. S. Lewis and meeting the woman who would eventually become his wife. These factors, combined with the revelation of *Perelandra*, restored Como's hope. Como interestingly applies the same critical eye to his own life as he does Lewis's works. In his chapter on Storytelling, Como unspools the literary and spiritual significance of *Perelandra* as perhaps autobiographical, and the larger significance of the Ransom Trilogy as more of a bildungsroman than a science fiction tale. In fact, Como argues that *Perelandra* engages three levels of belief: literary, imaginative, and spiritual. This, he writes, is what Wordsworth and MacDonald achieved for Lewis, and what Lewis now does for Como and many other modern readers. This spiritual level of belief is "conveyed by awe and marked . . . by holiness: we are fully immersed in the numinous" (Como borrowing language from Lewis's *The Problem of Pain*) (69). Thus, Como urges the reader to interpret *Perelandra* not only as a typical "outer space story" or a "good versus evil" homage, but as a metaphor for the critical spiritual battles fought on *this* planet. Como fully embraces the parallel that his journey is similar to Lewis and to his character Ransom, a fact which undergirds his premise that *Perelandra* can serve as a myth of spiritual development. Indeed, Como's book serves to illustrate Lewis's own belief in the integration of reason and imagination; the work itself serves to understand a story that resonates on multiple levels. Ultimately, Como's investigation is both entertaining and instructive.

Como's approach and exploration are a surprising twist in Lewis scholarship but a valuable addition to texts surrounding the impact of the science fiction trilogy. *Mystical Perelandra* is a testament to the transformative power of the written word.

CRYSTAL HURD
Northwind Theological Seminary

Paul Fiddes, *Charles Williams and C. S. Lewis: Friends in Co-inherence* (New York: Oxford University Press, 2021). 432 pages. $115.00. ISBN 9780192845467.

If shared merriment, as C. S. Lewis claims in "The Weight of Glory," "must be of that kind ... which exists between people who have, from the outset, taken each other seriously—no flippancy, no superiority, no presumption," surely shared theology should follow suit. In his book *Charles Williams and C. S. Lewis: Friends in Co-Inherence*, University of Oxford Professor Emeritus of Systematic Theology (and contributor of a number of insightful essays on the Inklings), Paul S. Fiddes does exactly that. In this study, which Rowan Williams has rightly called "a brilliant work," Fiddes pays Lewis and Williams the important, often-neglected compliment of taking these authors and their theologies seriously. By doing so, Fiddes's magisterial study accomplishes at least two critical tasks: it deepens and widens our knowledge about one of the most crucial friendships in the Inklings, and it explores key literary and theological concepts vital to that friendship.

Fiddes divides his book into five parts, the first three of which deal the most explicitly with Lewis and Williams's friendship and its intellectual implications; the final two sections explore the wider implications of the concept of co-inherence, considered in a specifically theological context. For most scholars of C. S. Lewis and admirers of the Inklings, these first three parts, "The 'Secret Road' of Friendship," "Ways of Exchange," and "A Collaboration in Co-Inherence," offer a treasure trove of helpful observations and analysis of the inception, growth, and implications of their friendship. The final two sections, "Further Studies in Co-Inherence" and "The Theology of Co-Inherence," go a long way to furthering Williams studies, and build on important work by Sørina Higgins and Grevel Lindop, among others.

The first three parts should prove most accessible to readers more familiar with Lewis in particular and the Inklings in general. Fiddes's painstaking and careful scholarship delves deeply into the origins and immediate impact of the friendship that quickly blossomed between Lewis and Williams in the late 1930s. Many biographers and scholars have cited the epistolary spark between the two authors, when Lewis wrote admiringly to Williams about his *The Place of the Lion* almost at the same time that Williams wrote to Lewis about *The Allegory of Love*, which Williams shepherded through Oxford University Press. Fiddes systematically explores the specific impact of that happy meeting, looking at the way Williams and Lewis in some ways shared and in others diverged sharply about the concept of romantic theology, a topic rightly attracting much study and attention of late. Fiddes traces their shared development regarding ideas about "the weight of glory," Williams's influence on *The Problem of Pain*, and the pair's key collaboration on Williams's Arthuraian poems. Fiddes accesses much unpublished material, including the work of Raymond Hunt, whose notebooks and other observations about Williams remain largely overlooked in the archives of the Marion E. Wade Center and the Bodleian Library. Fiddes's fine scholarship sets a bar for all other writers about the Inklings.

His sections concerning co-inherence (which many will recognize as the idea of "substitution" or "exchange" in the work and lives of both men) help readers to grasp the concept itself while tracing its evolution. Fiddes defines co-inherence as "the conviction that human persons inhere or dwell in each other so that they exist in a mutual interdependence, and that at the foundation of this relational reality the 'Persons' of a triune God permeate one another in love." This concept, which has perhaps not been explored deeply enough, offers a way of looking at these mythopoeic modernists within a deeply theological and theoretical context, and celebrates them in the seriousness and insightfulness of thoughtful analysis. Fiddes also traces the development of the romantic theology of both writers, noting how in both Lewis's Great Dance in *Perelandra* and *The Four Loves*, Lewis goes far to resolving his initial differences with Williams's ideas.

As with all excellent scholarship, even as this study poses important new queries, answers neglected questions, and provides new insight and new ways of thinking about the Inklings, some questions still linger. Notably, maybe even lamentably, one wonders why Fiddes's careful synthesis of a wide range of studies curiously omits the definitive, groundbreaking and essential work of Diana Pavlac Glyer; her books *The Company They Keep* and *Bandersnatch* offer genre-defining categories of collaboration that would have vastly helped the development of analysis in this already impressive work. While he rightly analyzes the importance of *The Four Loves* and provides a brief but helpful discussion of *Till We Have Faces*, a longer consideration of that last novel (which Lewis rightly called "far and away my best book") would add even more depth to the study. Nevertheless, *Charles Williams and C. S. Lewis: Friends in Co-Inherence* profoundly moves the landmarks of Inklings studies and offers an indispensable lens to anyone interested in a careful look at these and related writers. As a significant theologian and scholar, Fiddes pays these authors and their readers alike the grand compliment of taking them seriously, and by doing so, this book will surely widen many worlds.

ANDREW LAZO
Northwind Theological Seminary

Peter Grybauskas, *A Sense of Tales Untold: Exploring the Edges of Tolkien's Literary Canvas* (Kent, Ohio: Kent State University Press, 2021). $55.00. 176 pages. ISBN 978606354308.

With the September 2022 release of Amazon Prime's *Rings of Power*, Peter Grybauskas has selected an opportune time to explore the margins of Tolkien's legendarium. Perhaps, unlike the creators of the Amazon series, Grybauskas ventures to the edges of Middle-Earth with both scholarly rigor and faithfulness to the spirit of Tolkien's mythmaking project. With this powerful combination, Grybauskas makes a persuasive case for why we should consider the legendarium's "untold tales"—the "gaps, enigmas, allusions, digressions, omissions, ellipses, and loose ends that pepper [Tolkien's] narratives" (1)—as "a defining feature of his subcreation" (xx). While not necessarily groundbreaking in taking up this theme, the study illuminates how careful attention to the periphery of Tolkien's work sheds new light on both his literary techniques and broader cultural legacy.

A senior lecturer at the University of Maryland, Grybauskas takes the study's motivating question from a letter Tolkien wrote to his son Christopher in 1945, describing what Tolkien calls the "fundamental literary problem": "A story must be told or there'll be no story, yet it is the untold stories that are most moving" (1). How, then, does Tolkien tell the untold tales? And to what effect? Grybauskas gives a plethora of examples that quickly convey the depth and breadth of this phenomenon in Tolkien's oeuvre. First, we have the snatches of verse and legend about the Last Alliance we hear from characters as diverse as Samwise Gamgee, Elrond Half-Elven, and a pair of Orcs (26). Then, there is the story of Celebrimbor, original creator of the Rings of Power, who is mentioned only three times in *The Lord of the Rings. This is followed by* the epic deeds of Túrin Turambar, alluded to by Elrond when Frodo accepts the Ring and just once more after Sam defeats Shelob (50-1), and, perhaps most famously, Treebeard's tantalizing evocation of the missing Entwives (122). Grybauskas categorizes this "unfinished tangle of plotlines, developments, and movements" (73) into three major types: faded tradition, allusive web, and omission (21-5). His central claim is that these categories of untold tales work together to create the remarkable sense of depth and mythic history that "color, inform, and enrich the reading of [Tolkien's] work" (73).

Fittingly for the subject matter, Grybauskas brings deep background knowledge of the legendarium to his study. His sources range from Tolkien's classic stories and essays to personal correspondences, medieval scholarship (even an undergraduate essay on the *Kalevala*), and lesser-known manuscripts like *The Homecoming of Beorhtnoth Beorhthelm's Son*, Tolkien's dramatic-verse addition to the Old English *Battle of Maldon*. Grybauskas marshals this wide-ranging archive across five main chapters. The first draws mostly from Tolkien's 1939 essay "On Fairy-Stories" to flesh out the importance of the "fundamental literary problem" to his mythmaking project; the last explores the enduring legacy of Tolkien's untold tales in film, video games, and other pop culture adaptations. The three middle chapters develop the meat of Grybauskas's argument, showing with a series of close-readings how each of the three categories of untold tales develops the rich mythic history behind Tolkien's corpus: the allusions to the Last Alliance in *The Lord of the Rings* (chapter two), the faded tradition of the Túrin saga (chapter three), and omission in *The*

Homecoming of Beorhtnoth (chapter four). Throughout, Grybauskas moves smoothly between the legendarium's literary-technical minutiae and its large-scale mythopoetic mission. In one particularly moving section, Grybauskas demonstrates how Tolkien's use of parentheses and footnotes in referencing Túrin Turambar's story gives the reader a poignant sense of Middle Earth's lost history, calling her attention to the same problem of forgotten tradition that Tolkien so forcefully critiqued in his own age and set out to correct through his "mythology for England," in Humphrey Carpenter's memorable phrase (61).

Though several similar studies have emerged in the last fifteen years (3), *A Sense of Tales Untold* advances the discussion of Tolkien's "hidden depth" by taking a direction similar to that of Holly Ordway in her 2021 study, *Tolkien's Modern Reading*: namely, putting Tolkien in conversation with contemporary writers. Grybauskas explores how Tolkien's "untold tales" reflects and refracts similar techniques found in the work of other twentieth-century fantasy writers like Lord Dunsany and E.R. Eddison, as well as arch-modernist Ernest Hemingway (15). This comparative approach pays dividends in the fourth chapter, when Grybauskas makes a persuasive case for renewing scholarly attention to *The Homecoming of Beorhtnoth* by showing how the text mirrors Hemingway's "iceberg theory" to achieve its remarkable sense of depth (87). Furthering Ordway's work on Tolkien's contemporary sources, Grybauskas's analysis overturns the caricature of Tolkien as the long-winded "dinosaur." Not only does he borrow literary techniques usually considered modern, but he does so to convey maximal background in minimal words. The insight scores a hit against critics like Harold Bloom and Salman Rushdie, whom Grybauskas quotes in the introduction for reproaching Tolkien's "over-written" style (xviii).

This reframing of Tolkien as engaged with, if not wedded to, modernist literary techniques springboards the readers into the study's final chapter, where Grybauskas offers an illuminating discussion of how Tolkien's "untold tales" continue to influence contemporary fantasy. We hear of similar techniques in the work of George R.R. Martin and Ursula Le Guin (101-4), in the "slow gaming" style of role-playing video games like *Diablo* and *Dark Souls* (110-15), and in film adaptations of *The Lord of the Rings* and *The Hobbit*, which may be less emblematic of Tolkien's hidden depth more indicative of how *telling* too many untold tales can destroy the magic (104-110). Along the way, Grybauskas shows how close-reading these non-traditional media can push the edges of Tolkien scholarship into intriguing new territory.

If one can criticize Grybauskas for omission, *A Sense of Tales Untold* devotes disappointingly little attention to the philosophical and theological implications of Tolkien's "ice berg" techniques. How was Tolkien's hidden depth influenced by his Catholic faith, for example? How do the legendarium's deliberate lacunae leave room for readers to fill in narrative gaps with their own historical imagination and artistic sub-creation? These questions seem crucial for a full understanding of how Tolkien's mythopoetic project connects with his literary techniques, especially in light of his well-known regard for *The Lord of the Rings* as a "fundamentally religious and Catholic work," and his distaste for allegory as an affront to the freedom of the reader.[1] Perhaps in keeping with the spirit of his project, however, Grybauskas leaves these dimensions of Tolkien's tales untold for future scholars to explore.

Omissions notwithstanding, *A Sense of Tales Untold* is essential reading for scholars who want to understand Tolkien's literary methods, place Tolkien in conversation with other leading authors of the twentieth century, and better understand his ongoing legacy in the twenty-first. Grybauskas's study is also a fitting tribute to the late Christopher Tolkien, who devoted so much of his life to expanding the edges of his father's legendarium, as well as a hopeful argument that a deeper appreciation for Tolkien's tales untold may not only "lead us into new imaginative territory," but also "point us back to the story told with fresh eyes" (122).

LAUREN SPOHN
The University of Oxford

---

[1] J. R. R Tolkien, *The Letters of J. R. R. Tolkien*, ed. Humphrey Carpenter and Christopher Tolkien (Boston: Houghton Mifflin, 1981), 172; Tolkien, *The Lord of the Rings* (Great Britain: HarperCollins, 2003), xxvi.

Joel D. Heck, *No Ordinary People: 21 Friendships of C. S. Lewis* (Hamden, CT: Winged Lion Press, 2021). 384 pages. $19.50. ISBN 9781935688228.

People return to Lewis's narrative works not only for the snow-gilt lamppost, floating islands, and unbendable grass, but for the diverse assemblage of characters he depicts so well that one gets the impression he knew them. Once met, who can forget King Lune, MacPhee, the Fox, or Sarah Smith? Joel Heck's latest book, *No Ordinary People: 21 Friendships of C. S. Lewis,* does not get bogged down in trying to make one-to-one connections between Lewis's friends and his literary creations. In fact, Heck may be just about the only Lewis scholar who takes seriously the cautions in *The Personal Heresy,* an exchange that rails against interpreting literature through the author's biography. Instead, Heck explores a diverse array of Lewis's friendships revealing a cast of colorful characters who made an impression on Lewis, helping shape the man who would become the memorable author even as he influenced them.

Heck organizes the book into three major sections: "Side by Side Friends," "Opponents, but Friends," and "Co-workers and Fellow Pilgrims." Fellow Oxford apologist Austin Farrer and childhood friend Arthur Greeves fall under the first category. The secondary section features Arthur C. Clark, an atheist science-fiction author, as well as Alec Vidler who was a liberal theologian and magazine editor. Lastly, Oxford Socratic Club founder and chairman Stella Aldwinckle and former student Mary Neylan are found in the third category. Heck does not spend much time elaborating on the difference between "Side by Side Friends" and "Co-workers and Fellow Pilgrims," but the latter seems to be confined to relationships where Lewis was interacting more as a professional colleague (such as with Cambridge colleague, classicist Nan Dunbar), mentor, and even father figure (for Maureen Moore, the sister of Paddy Moore whose family Lewis agreed to look after when Paddy died in WWI). Mrs. Janie Moore is somewhat awkwardly placed in the first section, although the standards for inclusion are never quite laid out. Heck offers prior popularity of the relationships as reasons against including Tolkien, Williams, Barfield, Davidman, and Sayers, and yet Arthur Greeves, Warren Lewis, and Hugo Dyson are all included (5). The intentionally diverse cast may be meant to show that extraordinary people can be found where least expected.

Chapters are written such that they stand alone which occasionally leads to redundancies. For instance, the same event featuring multiple friends may be repeated in more than one chapter, as in the case of a dinner party featuring Nan Dunbar and Murial Bradbrook, described twice within six pages. The subject of each chapter, unfortunately, is not included at the header of each page. However, chapters often include a brief introductory section on how the subject of the chapter knew Lewis, a brief biography, an extended section on the relationship with Lewis, and a conclusion with reflections on the relationship and friendship in general, though these sub-sections vary. Chapters vary widely in length, from eight pages for Bradbrook to twenty-six devoted to C.E.M. Joad. Sister Penelope's thirty-page chapter is somewhat inflated by three appendices, listing her books, the date and subject of all of Lewis's letters to her, and a list of all the books and authors they discussed. In fact, you will find several chapters include appendices, as well as multiple pictures. The book's greatest virtue lies in fleshing out the picture of people whose names Lewis readers have likely heard but never truly known, while introducing new characters to fill in gaps. For example, a reader will learn Hugo Dyson "probably had a greater impact than Tolkien" on Lewis's conversion (34), that the famed "Do *you* like that?" meeting between Lewis and Arthur Greeves took place when the former was 15 and the latter 18, and that Mrs. Moore may have been unfairly characterized in scholarship due to overreliance on Warnie's criticisms and she may not have been an atheist when she died (105). Lewis's collegial, and at times deferential, relations with his female colleagues at Cambridge will challenge some stereotypes regarding Lewis, while his paternal/pastoral care for his former students and relations will make one appreciate the man's compassion even more. "Opponents but Friends" will likely garner the most interest. The fact that Lewis would lend his support to Arthur C. Clarke, who initiated correspondence with Lewis stating, "I wish to disagree, somewhat violently, with you" to help promote Clark's book *Childhood's End* is but one striking example of what friendship among those with striking disagreements can develop (202, 206).

A reader of Heck's work not only meets many interesting people, they meet many interesting sources. Heck mines the Lewis family papers, Lewis's letters, both Lewis brothers' diaries—including Warren's unpublished diary—oral histories, and direct contact with various legatees of the original subjects. For many of the friends, the basic biographical information comes from Walter Hooper's *Companion and Guide,* but

Heck also makes extensive use of the records and writings of the friends themselves. Heck employs all the various anthologies of memories of those who knew Lewis e.g., *Speaker and Teacher, At the Breakfast Table, C. S. Lewis Remembered*, and a broad assortment of secondary articles from publications ranging from *VII* to *Sehnsucht* to *CSL*, to *A Pilgrim in Narnia*.[1]

No Ordinary People is no ordinary book.[2] Its scope and scholarship immediately commend it as a go-to resource for Lewis scholars.[3] Its subject matter makes it of great interest in a world where meaningful friendships—friendships that challenge us and make us grow into better people—are typically few in number. How did Lewis do it? *No Ordinary People* will inspire readers to pursue their own friendships further and to seek friendship in unexpected persons. It will also likely leave readers wanting to check out a book by Warnie, Sister Penelope, or Arthur Clarke. Or perhaps another book by Joel Heck. When can he write the sequel?[4]

JOSIAH PETERSON
Chandler Preparatory Academy

Crystal Hurd, *The Leadership of C. S. Lewis: Ten Traits to Encourage Change and Growth* (Hamden, CT: Winged Lion Press, 2022). 232 pages. $18.99. ISBN 9781935688334.

In *The Leadership of C. S. Lewis*, Crystal Hurd makes a winsome case that C. S. Lewis was and is a leader. This case is based on a concept of leadership as influence. Other forms and understandings of leadership

---

[1] Frustratingly, the formatting of the citations is quite inconsistent, making them harder to navigate.

[2] Publisher, Winged Lion Press, has been on a roll lately with Lewis scholarship. See, for example, *The Undiscovered C. S. Lewis* edited by Bruce R. Johnson and *The Leadership of C. S. Lewis* by Crystal Hurd.

3 Lewis scholars already had much to be grateful for in Joel Heck's online publication, "Chronologically Lewis," a more than 1,000 page record of every known date of an event in Lewis's life, available at JoelHeck.com.

[4] Potential candidates for inclusion in a subsequent volume might include Fred Paxford, E.M.W. Tillyard, Ruth Pitter, Roger Lancelyn Green, William T. Kirkpatrick, and Douglas Gresham.

are acknowledged, but by leaning into the leadership as influence understanding, the case for viewing C. S. Lewis as a leader is unassailable, despite Lewis's own denials. Then having established Lewis as a leader, Hurd seeks to show how, from both a biographical and literary perspective, Lewis demonstrated and continues to demonstrate ten leadership traits.

The case for Lewis as a leader is winsome and strengthened by occasional explorations of how Hurd herself has been influenced by Lewis. Hurd makes it personal, for example, in talking about Lewis's courage when she acknowledges the scene of Reepicheep passing into Aslan's Country "nearly brings me to tears every time" (91-2). She also encourages her readers to make it personal by offering discussion questions at the end of each chapter. These discussion questions are a real strength of the book and encourage the book to be read in community.

However, the book would benefit by more clearly targeting the community it wants to engage. Is this a book for Christian fans of Lewis seeking to grow as leaders? Hurd seems to presume a Christian reader thus missing out on the opportunity to engage the broader audience Lewis himself commanded. At the same time, all are assumed to be leaders because everyone has influence, even though not everyone sees himself or herself as a leader (including Lewis) or desires to grow as a leader. It isn't clear how familiar one needs to be with leadership and the various approaches to and understandings of leadership to engage with the book. Similarly, it isn't clear how familiar one needs to be with both Lewis and his writings. The background of some of Lewis's books are provided and reiterated while looking at each leadership trait, but with other books much is presumed.

These aside, a Christian fan of Lewis will grow as a leader by examining and applying the lessons from Lewis's life and writings around each of the leadership characteristics considered. No rationale is provided as to why these particular traits were selected as opposed to others. Hurd acknowledges that "Duty is often an underrated aspect of leadership" (153) and that "creativity is an important, if often neglected, trait of successful leadership" (194). Nonetheless, the ten leadership qualities selected, including both duty and creativity, are evident in many effective leaders. They are also clearly evident in Lewis's life and writings as Hurd amply documents. Without being rigid in her approach, Hurd generally considers each of the leadership qualities covered through the lenses of the general literature on the traits, how Lewis's life demonstrated each one, his fictional depictions of them and in his nonfiction treatment of the traits.

Early in the work, Hurd links leadership to obedience (22) and goes on to refer to leadership as a "call" (23). This understanding contributes to the consideration of the leadership characteristic of duty as particularly noteworthy. Lewis himself attributes our actions to the motivation of either duty or pleasure (141-2). Yet in Christ, duty is transformed into a pleasure, and this is the case when it comes to the duty to grow as leaders. Examining *The Leadership of C. S. Lewis: Ten Traits to Encourage Change and Growth* is indeed a pleasant duty for all who have been influenced (led!) by Lewis and dutifully seek to grow themselves.

Jon Heeringa
First Presbyterian Church, Harrisonburg

Bruce R. Johnson, ed., *The Undiscovered C. S. Lewis: Essays in Memory of Christopher W. Mitchell* (Hamden, CT: Winged Lion Press, 2021). 389 pages. $24.99. ISBN 978193568813.

It may be tempting to believe that any new addition to the voluminous corpus of Lewis scholarship would either be hagiography or sheer redundancy. While that may certainly be true of a few outlying publications, it is difficult to argue the same for the latest volume of essays published in memory of the late Christopher W. Mitchell. This collection, *The Undiscovered C. S. Lewis: Essays in Memory of Christopher W. Mitchell*, is replete with insightful and illuminating discussions on Lewis the warfighter, communicator, and imaginative theologian (just a few of the traits and potentialities explored therein). While those aspects of Lewis's life and works may have been previously known, the "undiscovered" aspects of these essays stem from the unique perspective each contributor brings to light.

The book is divided into three main sections: Historical Studies, Assessments and Reassessments, and Interactions with Contemporaneous or Current Writers. In the first section, Grayson Carter's essay on Lewis's wartime experiences connects lines to some of the possible influences that those experiences had on his life, writings, and religious views. While it may be obvious that the war would have had its influence, Carter fleshes out some particulars that may set the fuller scope of what could have been lost had Lewis not faced that horrendous trial during a crucial period of his intellectual, spiritual, and physical journey. The ends do not justify the means of course, and Lewis would have certainly been spared a great deal of trauma if the Great War had not pulled him onto its hellish stage. But, in spite of this great evil, the war's effects on his literary achievements have made its readers all the wiser.

Turning to the theological in the Assessments and Reassessments section, Adam J. Johnson provides a fascinating argument that Lewis, famously reticent on theories of the atonement, implicitly conceived of a *Christus Victor* "turned inside out" (224) with the ransom of God through Christ also being a re-establishment of the earth within the harmony of the Cosmic Song. Johnson argues to his readers that while Lewis may have demurred in his correspondence and non-fiction writing, his unique theory of the atonement is present in his imaginative works, especially the Ransom Trilogy.

In the final section of the collection, Stephen Beebe demonstrates that Lewis's skills and intuitions as a communicator anticipated key focal points of Communication as a formal academic discipline far prior to those central tenets being codified (those focal points are still an ongoing conversation today). Not only was Lewis himself a skilled writer, orator, and communicator who freely gave advice on those pursuits when asked, but he also intuited that communication was central to the conveyance of *meaning* and how it is related across human relationships.

These are but a few of the eighteen total essays contained in this collection, and all of them enrich the reader with new insight, fresh reminders, and potentially new paths for others to clear as Lewis is juxtaposed with contemporary or current writers. Readers may have never met Christopher Mitchell, but many of the contributors to this volume knew him dearly. His absence is keenly felt, not only as one who contributed to the flowering field of Lewis scholarship, but as a missing variable in the "algebra of friendship" as Diana Glyer so beautifully puts it in her own essay. While the very application of algebraic methods is to "find" that variable, the analogy here breaks down because death has robbed us of our mathematical potency.

Lives and legacies such as Lewis's and Christopher Mitchell's remind us, who too frequently languish in Holy Saturday, that they are already a day ahead. Through Christ, Easter dawn approaches, and this collection by editor Bruce Johnson is a beautiful and valuable homage to that shared hope.

BRIAN C. RODEN
Northwind Theological Seminary

Joseph A. Kohm Jr., *The Unknown Garden of Another's Heart: The Surprising Friendship between C. S. Lewis and Arthur Greeves* (Eugene, OR: Wipf and Stock, 2022). 114 pages. $21.00. ISBN 9781666710403.

At slightly over a hundred pages and written in accessible language, Joseph Kohm Jr.'s *The Unknown Garden of Another's Heart: The Surprising Friendship between C. S. Lewis and Arthur Greeves* (2022) can easily be read in one sitting or two. The title is beautiful and suggestive of an image from Lewis's poem "To the Memory of Arthur Greeves" (1917)—which speaks of "Roaming—without a name—without a chart— / The unknown garden of another's heart."

The friendship between C. S. Lewis (1898–1963) and Arthur Greeves (1895–1966) is "surprising" because it lasted nearly fifty years and because Lewis was an intellectual who rose to international fame, while Greeves lived a more ordinary and seemingly unaccomplished life. And yet, as the author suggests (persuasively, I think), "it was Arthur Greeves—not Owen Barfield, not J.R.R. Tolkien, and not even Lewis's brother Warnie—who was C. S. Lewis's best friend" (3). All the hallmarks of deep friendship are there: common interests, honesty, vulnerability, and affection. In his nearly three hundred letters to Arthur, whom Lewis calls his "first friend," we find a Lewis who reveals his innermost thoughts and secrets. "You are my only real Father Confessor," he tells Greeves.[1] "I never pass a day without remembering you."[2] *The Unknown Garden of Another's Heart* will help

---

[1] Letter of 3 April 1930, in C. S. Lewis, *The Collected Letters of C. S. Lewis*, ed. by Walter Hooper, 3 vols. (San Francisco: HarperCollins, 2004–7), 1:186.

[2] Letter of 25 May 1941, in Lewis, *CL*, 2:487–8.

correct the popular misconception of Lewis's approach to friendship as somehow impersonal, secretive, and even snobbish.[3]

The author has consulted all the relevant primary sources. The most important primary source is of course *They Stand Together: The Letters of C. S. Lewis to Arthur Greeves (1914–1963)* (1979) edited by Walter Hooper, which includes the nearly three hundred letters from Lewis to Arthur, all four surviving letters from Arthur to Lewis, Warnie's handful of letters to Arthur, and Hooper's indispensable *Introduction, Editor's Note* and numerous helpful footnotes and minibiographies. Also consulted are Arthur Greeves's unpublished diaries, Lewis's pre-conversion diary *All My Road Before Me*, his autobiography *Surprised by Joy,* and several leading biographies of Lewis. The analytical yield of mining Arthur's diaries is surprisingly modest: a mere three paragraphs (7-8). Also, Lewis wrote long portraits of the Greeves family, and of Arthur Greeves in particular, that were published in *They Stand Together.* Walter Hooper proclaimed that these depictions were "perhaps as definitive a portrait as we are likely to come by."[4] It is a shame that Kohm refers to them so sparingly (6-7). They ought to have been reproduced in full. These missed opportunities point to the first of the work's major limitations.

The narrative is terribly one-sided. It reads more like a pastoral commentary on Lewis's life and faith than an original contribution to our understanding of Arthur Greeves or his "surprising friendship" with Lewis. We follow Lewis "in real time," reading page after page about things anyone who has ever read a biography of Lewis already knows all too well, occasionally dipping into his letters to Arthur. Chapter four ("First Friends") is almost entirely redundant: the first two-thirds chronicle Lewis's relationship with Mrs. Janie Moore and his friendships with Barfield, Cecil Harwood, Nevill Coghill, and Tolkien. Only a few letters survive from the long period covered in chapters six ("Homeliness") and seven ("A New Gap"); this is compensated by lengthy introductions of Lewis's other friends Alan Griffiths, Charles Williams, Sister Penelope, Dorothy Sayers, Ruth Pitter, and Joy Davidman. Chapter eight ("The Sword of Damocles")

---

[3] See Jason Lepojärvi, "Misreading C. S. Lewis on Friendship: The Charges of Sexism, Secrecy, and Snobbery," in *Theology Today* (forthcoming 2023).

[4] Walter Hooper, ed., *They Stand Together: The Letters of C. S. Lewis to Arthur Greeves (1914–1963)* (New York, NY: Macmillan, 1979), 24.

recounts the three deaths of Mrs. Moore, Joy, and Lewis. Ironically, the only death *not* covered in every biography of Lewis—namely, Arthur's—is completely forgotten.[5]

The author may have been overly optimistic in his belief that "we are able to reconstruct much of the content and subject matter . . . from Lewis's letter's alone" because he "habitually restated pertinent information from the last letter he received from the sender" (5). This device, or the author's exploration of these letters, allows us to gauge the "plot" of their friendship—what was discussed, what happened and when—but not so easily the "man." Who *was* Arthur Greeves? The garden of Arthur's heart remains largely unknown. His possible homosexuality is discussed almost on the very last page which is odd, especially given that "sexual proclivities" were discussed at length in chapter two and hinted at in chapter four's aside about Arthur's "nature" and "desires" (21-5, 47).

The second limitation pertains to the elusive target audience, and the work seems strangely mistargeted. If the audience is Christian (and probably Protestant Christian given the many pastoral exhortations and scriptural references), why explain basic Christian doctrines? If the audience is North American, of which "almost half of all Americans sometimes or always feel lonely" (113), why assume that they would catch the meaning of "Lewis's Boswell"? (35). Above all, if it is written for fans of Lewis, why tediously recount well known facts about his life and thought? Given that we already have Lewis's letters, diary, autobiography, and good biographies, Hooper took a different approach in *They Stand Together*: "It is not, I feel, necessary to give here many of the generally known facts of C. S. Lewis's life."[6] This book would have benefitted from Hooper's example.

Hooper declares: "The question [of who Arthur Greeves was] may never be answered satisfactorily until, and if, a biography of Greeves is attempted."[7] For the time being, *They Stand Together* remains the closest thing to a "biography" of Lewis's "first friend." For readers who either cannot find a copy of *They Stand Together* or roam through its five hundred pages, *The Unknown Garden of Another's Heart* is the only available alternative.

---

[5] It is beautifully recounted in Hooper's introduction to *They Stand Together*, 37–8.
[6] Hooper, *They Stand Together*, 13
[7] Hooper, *They Stand Together*, 12.

Perhaps it will encourage readers to proceed to primary sources and inspire scholars to compose a biography of Arthur Greeves.

JASON LEPOJÄRVI\
George Fox University

Louis Markos, *C. S. Lewis for Beginners*, illus. by Joe Lee (Danbury, CT: For Beginners, 2022). viii + 192 pages. $15.95. ISBN: 97819399940806.

A nonfiction graphic book series, "For Beginners" is designed to introduce young adults to various writers, thinkers, and subjects in a straightforward and accessible manner. Originally, its target audience was disadvantaged or struggling readers; its aim is to help them delve into complex topics with the hope of converting those near non-readers into readers. More recent additions to the series have focused on such writers as James Joyce, Marcel Proust, Toni Morrison, Ayn Rand, and J. R. R. Tolkien. *C. S. Lewis for Beginners* is the latest addition to this growing collection.

After a brief biography of Lewis in the first chapter, Louis Markos moves chronologically through the writings of C. S. Lewis, devoting one chapter each to exploring his various books. As Markos explains in the introduction, this pattern is broken in chapter three where four of his books on literary criticism are discussed in a single chapter: *The Allegory of Love, The Personal Heresy, English Literature in the Sixteenth Century*, and *Studies in Words*. Although "brilliant," these four "are a bit technical for the average reader" (6). Markos does not devote individual chapters to the essays, poems, or letters written by Lewis but draws upon all these while commenting on his other books.

Chapters two through twenty-eight each begin with a series of bullet points to help orient readers to the particular work or works being discussed. Through this staccato method, Markos not only explains the basic facts about each book, but also summarizes a surprising amount of scholarly discussion. For example, while examining *The Great Divorce*, Markos explains, "Lewis condenses the full weight of Dante's *Divine Comedy* into the space of 100 pages. His guide, George MacDonald, combines Dante's

Virgil and Beatrice" (92). On the composition of *Miracles*, Markos clarifies how:

> After Catholic philosopher Elizabeth Anscombe bested Lewis at a meeting of the Oxford Socratic Club on issues raised by *Miracles*, he revised Chapter three for the second edition (1960). Anscombe was satisfied by the changes, but the chapter is arguably the most obscure and difficult chapter in all of Lewis's work! (99)

Such information is followed by further prose commentary in an easily readable style. Over one hundred drawings by Joe Lee are particularly effective in illustrating various points in the text. These chapters conclude with what is perhaps the greatest virtue of *C. S. Lewis for Beginners*: "Suggested Pairings." Lewis's books are paired with essays by Lewis which are thematically connected. These are designed to spur beginning readers forward, but avid readers of Lewis will also find them useful. Likewise, the included annotated bibliography will be appreciated by both sets of readers.

In such a swift and condensed overview of the Lewis corpus, it is to be expected that the author occasionally makes misstatements. Lewis is praised for his supposed "thorough knowledge" of Hebrew (39) whereas Lewis was always dependent on others for insights into that language.[1] Markos retells the old myth that, during World War II, "Lewis's voice was the second most recognizable one on the radio after Winston Churchill's!" (22). However, any viewer of the 2010 movie *The King's Speech* would question the veracity of such a statement, plus an examination of the actual wartime ratings kept by the BBC Listener Research Department do not support such a claim.[2]

These minor flaws do not distract from Louis Markos's remarkable achievement of producing a short and reliable entry to C. S. Lewis for complete beginners. Introductions to Lewis and his writing are often

---

[1] "I have often wished I had time to learn Hebrew, but I think it would be for more an indulgence that a duty." Letter of 24 April 1936 to Dom Bede Griffiths, in C. S. Lewis, *The Collected Letters of C. S. Lewis*, ed. by Walter Hooper, 3 vols. (San Francisco: HarperCollins, 2004-7), 2:186.

[2] See Bruce R. Johnson, "C. S. Lewis and the BBC's *Brains Trust*: A Study in Resiliency," in *SEVEN: An Anglo-American Literary Review*, 30 (2013), 80.

lacking in either quality, accessibility, or brevity. Markos has avoided all these pitfalls in a succinct and wide-ranging volume.

BRUCE R. JOHNSON
Scottsdale, Arizona

John Rosegrant, *Tolkien, Enchantment and Loss: Steps on the Developmental Journey*. (Kent, Ohio: Kent State University Press, 2022). 220 pages. $58.99. ISBN 9781606354353.

John Rosegrant's *Tolkien, Enchantment, and Loss* is an excellent and highly recommended book for readers wanting to delve into the psychological depths of J.R.R. Tolkien's Legendarium. Using an "approach" (8) influenced and guided (6, 8) by psychoanalysts Sigmund Freud, D.W. Winnicott, and Julia Kristeva, Rosegrant carefully and thoughtfully considers how themes of enchantment and loss pervade the Legendarium while suggesting some connections with Tolkien's own history.

Rosegrant's writing is exceptionally accessible. Although a desire to learn about Tolkien and psychology is required to enjoy the work, knowledge of either is not required to engage the text as Rosegrant succinctly summarizes both psychological concepts and story plots. In fact, *Tolkien, Enchantment, and Loss* could serve as a Rosetta Stone for Tolkien enthusiasts aspiring to explore developmental psychology as well as for students of psychology desiring to engage Tolkien. Rosegrant masterfully weaves both psychological concepts and illustrations from the Legendarium together in a cohesive and convincing manner while engaging other scholarly works. His knowledge of Tolkien's Legendarium and other works is laudable and Rosengrant's treatment of the text is exemplary; Rosegrant never forces concepts upon the text or reads the text in a flippant manner, but rather takes the stories written by Tolkien seriously, referencing them in a way that demonstrates integrity and a thorough understanding of the text.

Chapter one discusses Hobbits as symbols of childhood as the halflings are plunged into the more enchanting world of Middle-earth

(25): "This pair of tensions signified by the way the hobbits gradually increase their engagement with the enchanted world—the tension between childhood and adulthood, and the tension between enchantment and the ordinary—can be understood as two facets of the developmental need to surrender and transform childhood enchantments" (25). In Chapter two, intriguingly entitled "My Mother She Killed Me, My Father He Ate Me," Rosegrant explores Tolkien's "appreciation" for the dark fairy-tale "The Juniper Tree," as referenced in his essay "On Fairy Stories" (32). He notates the function of the "uncanny" in the tale: "The cannibalism of 'The Juniper Tree' balances precariously between enchantment and disenchantment . . . the uncanny image of the benign cannibal father points to possible enchantment by disordering us from reality; the fairy-tale form lets us situate the cannibalism more firmly in enchantment, but still with a degree of unease" (41). Chapter three is an intriguing comparison of Bilbo Baggins and the Master of Laketown, noting the contrast of how both characters handle the "invitations to enchantment" (49), while chapter four is an outstanding treatment of the abject in *The Hobbit* as Rosengrant considers Bag End, Bilbo, Gollum, and Smaug. The reader is struck by how artfully and intuitively Tolkien was able to address these deep issues as Rosengrant adds yet another layer to the rich patina of the Legendarium.

Chapter five, entitled "Mother Music," addresses the "cycles of disruption and repair" present through the music in the Legendarium (69) and makes a significant turn towards looking beyond the text at Tolkien himself. Here was the potential for Rosengrant to slip into presumptuous conjecture, but the author navigates Tolkien's biographical details with due humility and familiarity with source material. Chapter six compares and contrasts the feminine extremes of Galadriel and Shelob, while chapter seven takes a thoughtful look into Galadriel's Mirror. Rosengrant writes:

> Tolkien has intuitively given life to the ideas of Winnicott and Lacan that seeing oneself reflected develops identity, and that this structuring can either bring one closer to the truth (Winnicott) or alienate one from truth (Lacan). Frodo and Sam . . . in the Mirror of Galadriel . . . see alternate versions of themselves and have to choose which to actualize. (110)

Chapter eight looks at how Tolkien used his writing of the "Downfall of Númenor" therapeutically to address his fears of hubris and move into "transitional space" (118). Chapter nine, entitled "Something Has Gone Crack," takes a sobering look at how war trauma compounded Tolkien's early experiences of loss and how Tolkien expressed this loss in multiple places throughout the Legendarium. Chapter nine explores the mysterious Tom Bombadil as a transitional character unaffected by the One Ring which is "a fetish symbol" (118). Chapter eleven reflects on Tolkien's "Late Life Loss of Transitionality" (164). In the Epilogue, Rosegrant writes that, "On one level his Legendarium, with its pervasive theme of loss, may be understood as Tolkien's creative attempt to work through the tragedies of his life and stay in touch with hope and meaning.... But more importantly, the personal issues that Tolkien was dealing with were issues that everyone deals with" (174).

Brilliantly written, grounded in a profound knowledge of the source material, and teeming with fresh insights into Tolkien's beloved Legendarium, John Rosengrant's *Tolkien, Enchantment, and Loss* is a highly recommended read for anyone interested in delving deeper into the works of J.R.R. Tolkien.

JESSICA F. LEE
Northwind Theological Seminary

Harry Lee Poe, *The Completion of C. S. Lewis: From War to Joy (1945-1963)*, (Wheaton, IL: Crossway, 2022), 352 pages plus notes and index, $34.99, ISBN 9781433571022.

In the third and final installment of his biographical journey of C. S. Lewis, Harry Lee Poe returns to the whimsical and accessible sojourn through the final years of Lewis's life. Poe continues to delight readers with his thorough investigation of all aspects of Lewis's life. This final volume focuses on Lewis's rise in popularity and fame, his legions of fan mail, his developing friendships with various individuals, including poet Ruth Pitter, Lewis's eventual migration to a Chair at Cambridge, his brother's ongoing struggle with alcohol, his two marriages to Joy Davidman, and his eventual retirement, decline, and death.

While many would argue that there are *enough* Lewis biographies on the market, Poe continues to distinguish his work from other biographies through his consistent use of detailed research. Poe takes an extra step, illustrating to his audience the context of Lewis's actions and writings. This additional information adds a new layer to previous research that has been presented, perhaps ad nauseam, in other books over the last few decades. One example is Poe's erudite discussion of the "Zernov Group," an involvement that developed after Lewis's association in the Oxford Socratic Club. Lewis and Austin Farrer, along with several other Inklings, attended a meeting on Saturday evening hosted by Nicholas Zernov, an Orthodox theologian who wished to reconcile the relations between the Church of England and Orthodoxy. The club came to be known as the Fellowship of Saint Alban and Saint Sergius.[1] Most books gloss over this interesting involvement or ignore it altogether. While it may seem a footnote in Lewis's overall biography, it proves Lewis's consistent commitment to bring those of different backgrounds and faiths together—as *mere Christians*.

One aspect of Poe's work that continues in this volume is Poe's unfailing sense of humor. Poe recalls the two women who claimed to be Lewis's wife. He also discusses lukewarm responses that many of Lewis's friends had to Joy Davidman, as well as the fact that "Jack should have married Ruth Pitter." Virgil was a fine guide for Dante, and Poe is an astute and forthcoming escort through the experiences and proclivities of Lewis's life.

Poe also has a keen sense of Lewis's developing and evolving perspectives on a variety of topics, illustrating how early works, such as *The Allegory of Love*, contributed to later books such as *Spencer's Images of Life*. This is one of the great strengths of Poe's narrative: the three books together illustrate the ebb and flow of ideas and how Lewis navigated and artistically responded to these alterations. This includes the now-infamous Socratic Club exchange with Elizabeth Anscombe. Poe addresses how this interaction has been misinterpreted in other biographies—namely those authored by A. N. Wilson and Alister McGrath—yet, as Poe highlights, Anscombe did not disagree with Lewis on the idea, but rather his *expression* of the idea that naturalism is self-refuting. Poe also briefly comments on Michael Ward's thesis in *Planet Narnia* and digs deeper into Lewis's refusal to embrace Catholicism. Poe does not shrink from controversial topics but

---

[1] Alban was the first British Christian martyr, and Sergius was a "venerated Russian Orthodox monk" (117).

sees all aspects composing the sum of Lewis's journey.

Once again, Poe delivers a satisfactory reading experience with *The Completion of C. S. Lewis*. Poe's clear insight, unwavering devotion to quality research, and innovative narration make these books a library staple for any Lewis fan or scholar. Poe remains an entertaining and informative guide into many aspects of Lewis's life that others ignore or dismiss. His final section, which outlines what Lewis teaches us through his life and works, is the perfect conclusion to Poe's trio of biographies. Poe's literary approach is fair and balanced, weighed and reasoned, much like Lewis himself.

CRYSTAL HURD
Northwind Theological Seminary

James Prothero. *Sunbeams and Bottles: The Theology, Thought, and Reading of C. S. Lewis*. (Hamden, CT: Winged Lion Press, 2022). 442 pages. $22.99. ISBN 9781935688327.

James Prothero has been teaching, contemplating, and otherwise living with C. S. Lewis for a very long time. In his new book on Lewis, this dedication shows. *Sunbeams and Bottles* reads like a collection of thoughts gathered in notebooks over decades, waiting for the moment they would be gathered together into a comprehensive study of a single author whom the writer of this book has rightly obsessed over for a lifetime.

The contents of the book alternate between numbered chapters on a variety of topics and "Key Idea" chapters enumerated by the Greek alphabet. It took a few chapters to realize that the numbered and "Key Idea" chapters are not directly correlated, at which point I realized that the alternating approach allows the reader time to digest what is being covered. This means, though, that readers must choose how they want to use this book: a text to read cover to cover or one to use as a reference for specific topics. The numbered chapters include content on Lewis defying the categories of thought of those who try to appropriate him to their causes, placing Lewis in his philosophical and theological historical context, ideas central to Lewis's theology, people central to Lewis's life and thinking, the "mereness" of Lewis's Christianity, Lewis's literary theory, and his take on a variety of twentieth-century hot topics which are still relevant today. The "Key Idea" chapters include content on the nature of morality, truth, hell, prayer, predestination and free will, joy, being less than human, the necessity of paradox, imitation, and adoration, plus much more.

While this book has much to enjoy, there are a few criticisms which must be addressed. The first can be covered quickly enough. Prothero spends a great deal of time discussing Lewis's concept of Romanticism. However, when he turns to *Pilgrim's Regress* to discuss the topic, he leaves out Lewis's clearest definition of Romanticism which appears in the Afterword.

The author claims that Owen Barfield's "thesis" in *Poetic Diction* is "that all language is a growth and development of frozen metaphors" (147). Prothero mentions this idea at least one more time in saying, "language is made up of frozen metaphors from the past" (136), and also describes it as "Barfield's concept of language as originating with comparisons" (273). In his own summary of *Poetic Diction*, however, Barfield claims his central thesis to be about the emergence of poetic language from earlier stages of language and from the poetic imagination, and that from this understanding we gain proof for the "evolution of consciousness" (*Barfield* 29-30). It is true that in his wonderful essay, "Bluspels and Flalansferes," Lewis emphasizes the emergence of literal language from forgotten metaphors, but this is not Barfield's emphasis at all. Barfield's claim is that of "semantic unities," wherein all meanings in language, including literal and figurative, as well as subjective and objective, conscious and unconscious, abstract and concrete, and even the distinction between sign and signified, were present in the earliest languages as singular, united meanings. The very distinction between metaphor and literal statements didn't exist, and so "frozen metaphors" or "language originating in comparisons" would have been impossible early in the development of language.

Chapter twenty, "Educated by Joy: Lewis' Maturing Understanding of Women," was my least favorite section. First of all, Prothero builds an argument out of some very interesting detective work regarding Lewis's relationship with a woman named Vida Wiblin. However, I think he makes too much of this in his reading of Lewis's later life under the assumption that his conclusions about Wiblin and Lewis are true. My main problem with the chapter is that it reads like an indictment against Lewis for having twentieth-century views about women, which don't match up to twenty-first-century standards.

In chapter eight of *Sunbeams*, Prothero takes up the relationship between imagination and truth. He rightly notes differences between Lewis and Barfield on the issue, and indicates that for Lewis, the relationship between imagination and truth is problematic. Other Lewis scholars have wrestled with that. This author's solution, however, is inaccurate. Though he points out the importance of Reality in Lewis's total epistemology, Prothero fails to capture the full range of Lewis's definitions of truth, confuses Lewis's use of the word meaning, and misses when he tries to find the right relationship between reason and imagination.

The biggest problem with *Sunbeams and Bottles* is that it needs better editing, both in content and form. In form, it is a text with too many typos for an author to want in his book, including one that ruins a joke (instead of the OHEL we get the OHE [221]). It also has some needless repetition that a content editor would have likely removed. In content, it is a book that needed someone to point out the little mistakes. For instance, the author mentioned Digory's statement, "It's all in Plato!" was made in *The Lion the Witch and the Wardrobe* (173) when it only appears in *The Last Battle*. Another example is the fact that "Spencer" is actually spelled "Spenser" (220). A content editor would have also encouraged the author to break up his book into two or three separate volumes. *Sunbeams and Bottles* reads as the culmination of a lifetime of work in which the author wants to place everything he has to say about C. S. Lewis, but this is a mistake. Prothero's book is about Lewis in his intellectual times, the way people co-opt Lewis for their own purposes, and Lewis's most important ideas. The author tries to do too much, and the result is a book that doesn't do several things well enough.

On the other hand, Prothero's text also has many strengths. Prothero takes risks and makes bold claims. He forces the reader to think about Lewis in new ways: to consider that Lewis's primary mode of thought is narrative not systematic, to look at Lewis in light of the Victorian and Edwardian worlds in which he lived, to meditate on the possibility that, though Lewis was against the personal heresy, he may have been guilty of committing it on himself! Prothero takes scholars to task in pointing out that Lewis was not as pro-imagination as we have made him out to be. He speculates on diverse ideas like how Lewis's poetic style may have improved after his wife's death (161), the way Penelope Lawson's *The Wood for the Trees* may have impacted *Mere Christianity*, and why Lewis's understanding of the Catholic Church is of that Church as it existed before 1622.

Prothero's central thesis, that we can't pigeonhole Lewis, is strong. The categories we wish to impose on Lewis in theology (conservative vs. liberal, Catholic vs. Protestant), or politics (conservative vs. liberal vs. libertarian, capitalist vs. socialist), are just that—impositions, not the real thought of C. S. Lewis. Our author offers detailed proof of all failures to capture Lewis's sunbeams in their personal bottles.

The author's knowledge of philosophy, theology, and literary criticism is encyclopedic—it is an education especially in twentieth-century thought. I learned more new material from Prothero's work comparing Lewis's thought to that of contemporary theologians (like Barth and Vidler), and from his placing Lewis's literary criticism in the context of his times, than from any other chapters in the book. I find his claim that Lewis and Tolkien represent a Romantic counter-cultural response to their times to be another of the bolder statements which Prothero forces me to think through. Not to mention, his complete re-reading of postmodernism should be something all Christians give deep thought to.

A number of additional highlights are worth noting: Prothero's reading of *The Great Divorce* is very good. His emphasis on the importance of free will in Lewis's thinking is, I think, far too absent from what has been written about Lewis's theology. His study of magic (99-104) is first rate. He rightly reads the results of the Lewis/Anscombe debate, including blasting the lie that Lewis wrote no other apologetical works after that time (what of *The World's Last Night*?). He also emphasizes Lewis's ideas of "Clear versus Thick Religion" and "The Sin of Encore"—these ideas deserve more attention from Lewis scholars. What he says about Lewis's concept of Joy is unique. Chapter sixteen, "Lewis to Leavis to Foucault to Derrida" may be the best chapter in the entire book—an excellent help for all of us who still struggle with modern and post-modern literary critical theory.

James Prothero has given us new insights into C. S. Lewis. We can't ask much more in an age when Lewis is a staple of the publishing industry. What else can be said about him? Prothero's answers to that question can be found in *Sunbeams and Bottles*. However, he gives us even more: he comments on the ways in which we who love Lewis are reading ourselves into him rather than Lewis into us. Prothero gives us a book that *can* be consulted as a reference for years to come. I argued above that there is too much in it, yet that also means that there is much we can return to. He writes for both scholars and a general audience. Thus, the book is a good resource for all Lewis aficionados. Prothero's book is a corrective for and a warning to all of us who have been guilty of a kind of Lewisolatry—a kind that turns him into the Christian we need him to be for our own causes.

CHARLIE W. STARR
Alderson Broaddus University

Max MacLean as C. S. Lewis, in *The Most Reluctant Convert*.

Film Review

The Most Reluctant Convert: The Untold Story of C. S. Lewis, by Max MacLean, directed by Norman Stone, starring Max MacLean and Nicholas Ralph. New York City, NY: Fellowship for Performing Arts, 2021, 1 hr., 13 min.

The Fellowship for Performing Arts premiered a new film in 2021 about C. S. Lewis entitled *The Most Reluctant Convert: The Untold Story of C. S. Lewis*. It is a wonderfully entertaining movie that provides a revealing portrait of the great man and his fascinating faith journey. The movie features the superb actor Max McLean as the mature Lewis, the story's narrator. McLean is also the executive producer, along with Norman Stone. Certainly, McLean's fingerprints are all over this production, and his touch is deft. The movie was originally intended to have a one-night limited theatrical release in over 400 cities, but it proved to be popular, exceeding the critics' expectations. Due to positive reactions from audiences, it was given an extended theatrical run of fifteen additional days. The film is now available through Amazon on disc, on-line streaming, and digital download.

The casting is excellent. The lead role is played by Max McLean, who has portrayed Lewis in a number of stage productions: *The Screwtape Letters* (which began in 2008), The *Most Reluctant Convert* in 2016, and *Further Up, Further In* in October 2022. With warmth and candor, Max McLean projects an accessible C. S. Lewis that immediately draws us in.

McLean humanizes C. S. Lewis and makes his faith journey and intellectual maturation credible. For him to emulate Lewis's deep tonality and Irish-tinged Received Pronunciation would be virtually impossible, but he does a credible job diction. McLean's inflections and phrasing, coupled with his poetic style of enunciation, reflects Lewis's actual manner of speaking. The dialogue is effective—not just the words that comprise the script, but the words as articulated by Max McLean. One never has the sense that this is an actor "playing" C. S. Lewis, for Max McLean quickly establishes that he is C. S. Lewis. Welshman Richard Harrington plays Albert Lewis, a superb choice. He plays Lewis's father exactly as I envision him. Nicholas Ralph, from the Scottish Highlands (seen in the lead role in the PBS production "All Creatures Great and Small"), was thoroughly engaging as the young Lewis. The movie depicts the influence that William T. Kirkpatrick had on the young Lewis's mind far better than the one-man stage play could possibly do. To that end, Scotsman David Gant played William T. Kirkpatrick to a "T."

Max McLean (and other writers) did a masterful job of weaving together disparate thoughts from different books. The dialogue is intellectually engaging, emotionally moving, and humorous. Most of the script comes from four writings—*Surprised by Joy, The Problem of Pain, Mere Christianity*, and the sermon, "The Weight of Glory." McLean also draws from *Collected Letters* and from a few shorter essays in *God in the Dock, Present Concerns* and *Christian Reflections*. McLean begins the dialogue with a lengthy monologue extracted mostly from the Introduction of *The Problem of Pain*. It sets the stage for what is to follow and frames some of the questions this "weltanschauung voyager" was to face. Moreover, it establishes the subject's piercing intellect right from the get-go. McLean weaves phrases from various sources into this riveting opening monologue. For example, he makes a seamless transition from *The Problem of Pain* to an extract from *Surprised by Joy*. Even experienced Lewis readers will not likely note the mixed and intermingled sourcing. It works exceedingly well.

McLean cleverly weaves a tapestry of textual extracts from various sources. In a way, they seem to serve different purposes. The background context comes from *The Problem of Pain*. The compellingly rational arguments—such as "The Trilemma" and "the Argument from Desire"—come from *Mere Christianity*. And the best part, the imaginative lines, come from what many consider to be Lewis's most eloquent and imaginative writing which is the sermon, "The Weight of Glory."

The storyline for *The Most Reluctant Convert* is essentially gleaned from *Surprised by Joy*. The screenplay effectively introduces the dismay Lewis felt about his accepting confirmation and taking his first communion as a total nonbeliever. The story incorporates the young Lewis's loss of faith and growing atheistic leanings, sufficient to reveal the mindset of a young and committed skeptic. It paints a clear picture of the intellectual barriers the "faith journeyman" would have to overcome. The opening sequence, like Lewis's later conversion, is unexpected. Max McLean seamlessly steps from the world of acting and film production, into a wholly different world of C. S. Lewis's faith journey. It was rather like transitioning from the world of Shakespeare to the world of Hamlet—an analogy Lewis uses in the script. Another technique used by the producer was to insert the mature Lewis into a number of scenes from the past in close proximity to the young Lewis. All in all, the staging was very effective.

It is interesting to note that the telling of the story where a young Lewis happened upon *Phantastes*, a book by George MacDonald, is precisely at the center of the film. That is entirely appropriate, for this unanticipated discovery of "holiness" was central to Lewis's faith journey. It was at this point that the young Lewis, who had been steadily moving away from Christianity, began to turn back in the direction of his childhood Christian roots, though the return trip would be lengthy and labyrinthine. Also in the center of the film, we find a discourse on "desire." This, too, is fitting, as this was paramount in Lewis's growing awareness of something "further up, further in." Additionally, there is a scene featuring Lewis debating the rationality of cognition with Owen Barfield. This is important, not only because it led Lewis to realize that materialism was inadequate, but also because it gives the viewer a glimpse of the brilliance of Owen Barfield. Barfield was a great friend whose influence upon Lewis was as great as any other person with whom he associated while at Oxford.

Certainly, there is much more to the story that Lewis aficionados would find interesting. For example, the full gamut of Lewis's faith journey is only partially revealed. While the movie conveys how the young man moved from Christianity to materialism, to occultism and to idealism, there were steps along this journey that are not fully explained. The "New

Look" (Enlightenment Rationalism) that ruled over Oxford immediately after the Great War, and George Berkely's Immaterial Idealism, might have warranted a few minutes of attention. The movie does introduce the "argument from desire," but has nothing to say about the other arguments, such as the argument from morality, the argument from reason, or the argument from the numinous. A bit more about "joy" and "Sehnsucht" would be nice.

This film will be loved by Lewis experts and aficionados alike. But, in a way, I consider it to be ideal for Lewis neophytes. This film might be considered a central component in a comprehensive knowledge set about C. S. Lewis. Readers new to the works of C. S. Lewis would be well-advised to undergird their initial readings of Lewis's works with a solid foundation on the "untold story" of C. S. Lewis. With this beautiful movie, they will see Lewis in an entirely new light.

JAMES A. MOTTER
Suwanee, Georgia

Theater Review

The Lion, the Witch and the Wardrobe, based on the book by C. S. Lewis, directed by Mike Fentiman (based on the original production by Sally Cookson). Produced by Elliott and Harper Productions, and Catherine Schreiber. London, UK: Gillian Lynne Theatre, 30 October, 2022.

A new adaptation of *The Lion, the Witch and the Wardrobe*, first brought to the stage in Leeds by Sally Cookson, then toured by director Mike Fentiman, arrived at the Gillian Lynne Theatre in the West End in the summer of 2022. Previous adaptations include those by Glyn Robbins (RSC, 1998), Joseph Robinette (1989), Don Quinn (1968), and an off-Broadway one-act production by le Clanché du Rand (2011). Like them, Fentiman's version both adds and omits material (saddest of all was the omission of Mrs. Beaver's sewing machine), and thereby offers new insights into Lewis's classic tale as well as deviating in ways which startle us out of our own ideas about the text, as all adaptations ought to do.

There are some similarities and alterations in this production which deviate from previous depictions of *The Lion, the Witch, and the Wardrobe*. Like the 2005 film, this production figures Edmund (Shaka Kalokoh) as "bad" from the outset.[1] Grumpy and petulant, he seems set apart from his siblings on the train journey out of London. This sets up his humbling recognition of his treachery. It also, of course, makes clear the distinctions between Edmund and Lucy (especially their responses to Narnia) for younger audience members or anyone encountering the story for the first time. Damning him from the start felt rather unfair; after all, we are all rather more like Edmund than Lucy (Delainey Hayles). As the production progresses, it is clear that this facilitates later cuts such as the incredible speeding up of time. The Pevensies, for example, barely seem to settle into the Professor's (Johnson Willis) house before the children are all off to Narnia. This accelerated movement is explicitly visualized by designer Tom Paris's monumental clockface which dominates the set.[2]

Perhaps this production is most indebted to the stage adaptations of *The Lion King* (1997) and Michael Morpurgo's *War Horse* (2007) because of its skillful embracing of puppetry, most obviously in Aslan who had both puppet (Oliver Grant, Sean Lopeman and Shaun McCourt) and human (Chris Jared) form. This dual nature may suggest a gesture towards the God/man whom Aslan represents for some, although this should not be overemphasized since the production makes much of the pagan as well as the Christian imagery Lewis weaves into Narnia. More importantly, perhaps, to push this too far is to misread, since Aslan in puppet form is also very much *not* God-like. He seems inherently mutable rather than unchanging; the "un-puppeted" Aslan faces his stone-table sacrifice more

---

[1] In the Walt Disney/Walden Media adaptation directed by Andrew Adam-son, Edmund is figured as an unthinking (although unthinking due to deep grief, rather than necessarily intentional vindictiveness) young boy whose sadness in coping with the absence of his father (away fighting) and later further forced distancing from his mother leads him to rush back amidst an air raid for a portrait of his father. Even as the audience are invited to sympathize with this action, they are also called upon to criticize it—not for Edmund endangering his own life, but rather for the risk he then puts his older brother Peter in as he comes to rescue him as bombs fall in Blitz-ridden London.

[2] The space where the clock resides also later transforms into a stone table space where Aslan is (almost off-stage) killed by the White Witch.

like a deer caught in the headlights than a messiah drinking a foreordained divine "cup" of suffering.

Two other puppets are especially notable. Both are additions to the story, but they draw out further meanings already latent in Lewis's text: Schrödinger the cat and the cubistic illuminated dancing Turkish Delight, recalling Henri Matisse's L'Escargot (1953) but with added movement and neon pink glow. Played by puppeteer Oliver Grant, Schrödinger (the Professor's cat) was a striking comic addition to the story, and, I'd like to think, it was an intentional sly nod to the reality that Lewis and Noble Prize winner Erwin Schrödinger's paths really did cross at Magdalen.[3] Although it was the *cat* who was explicitly named "Schrödinger" throughout, both the Austrian accent of the *Professor* and the fact that Susan was reading Schrödinger's book *What is Life?* (1944) during the production, hint that the Professor himself was Schrödinger. Schrödinger's presence in the play brought his famous cat quantum superposition paradox (1935) into dialogue with Lewis's wardrobe and the question of what might be seen beyond their respectives frames. Both may contain more than one reality, but its presence is questionable until one opens the door; until that moment, it is potentially both there and not there.[4]

Edmund's encounter with the Turkish Delight offered a fascinating dramatization of Mr. Beaver's assessment that Edmund "had the look of one who has been with the Witch and eaten her food." As Edmund journeyed towards Cair Paravel, his stomach (and slowly his whole body) began to convulse as he regurgitated huge luminous cubes of Turkish Delight which then multiplied with Turkish Delight cuboid puppets onstage slowly forming a humanoid form. Although at some level this was simply a nod to the sickly sweet squidginess of Turkish Delight, this physicalization of his guilty conscience, and his gradual sickening realization that he had

---

[3] On the same day Schrödinger's election was marked (November 9, 1933) he received a telegram notifying him that he would receive the 1933 Nobel Prize in Physics [with Paul Diras]. For more on Schrödinger and his time at Magdalen see David C. Clary, *Schrödinger in Oxford* (Singapore: World Scientific Publishing, 2022), who notes that amongst those who "voted in three-quarter majority" for his election was one by the surname "Lewis," 74.

[4] Schrödinger's cat quantum superposition paradox was a thought experiment conceived of in dialogue with Einstein and written primarily to illustrate the problems he had with the Copenhagen interpretation of quantum mechanics.

been poisoned by the evil he had eaten, also provided a rich exploration of Edmund and his fight with and against the evil control of all "under her thumb." Racked with stomach-squirming and conscious-burning pain, his road to redemption commenced, and while still under the control of the White Witch, he began to painfully expel her influence away from himself.

Also worthy of mention are the ever-lovable Beavers (Julian Hoult and Christina Tedders), particularly this adaptation's self-chastising Mr. Beaver and, added in this production, his catchphrase "Deep Sorrow," expressing belief that he has once again misunderstood or failed. Among other magical pleasures, the play features fantastic music and choreography, full of scenes with talking animals dancing and carrying cellos and double basses.

The White Witch (Samantha Womack) faces Aslan (Chris Jared) in the London production of *The Lion, the Witch and the Wardrobe*.

The audience represented an impressive cross-section of ages from the very young to those who had grown to love fairy stories again, and the production seemed pitched to such a cross-section. Occasionally, however, there were choices which were rather more "adult" and indeed at odds with Lewis's text, such as the sadomasochistic spiked costumes of the White Witch's (Samantha Womack) evil followers. Presumably this was intended as a further indication of their evil, but the overly eroticized costumes seemed excessive. Evil was already evident in the Witch's camp without embodying it in this way, particularly when considering younger audience members for whom the White Witch alone and her commanding presence seemed evil enough. On the other hand, the decision to cast adult actors for the Pevensies did not negatively affect the childlike qualities of their characters, and the cast doublings (especially the Professor/Father Christmas, the White Witch/Mrs. Macready, Maugrim/White Stag) are bound to provoke further discussions. On a broader scale, the culturally diverse cast delivered a magical performance. Ultimately, this was an adaptation which pointed beyond as well as back to Lewis's *The Lion, the Witch and the Wardrobe* text, inviting us to see more of the wonder of a world which might be there (see Schrödinger) for those who have eyes to see it.

SARAH WATERS
University of Buckingham

Miscellaneous

Sehnsucht: The C. S. Lewis Journal Submission Guidelines

Sehnsucht: The C. S. Lewis Journal welcomes submissions of articles, review essays and announcements related to C. S. Lewis and his writings from all interested parties in (but not limited to) the following disciplines: history, literary studies and criticism, philosophy, theology, apologetics, biography, imagination, mythology, ethics, Christian spirituality, comparative religion, cultural studies, geography, rhetoric, and philology (broadly defined). *Submissions should embody original research or critical study and should not be under simultaneous consideration for publication elsewhere, either in the same or modified form.* Length of articles may vary from approximately 3,000 to 10,000 words (longer with the concurrence of the General Editor). Book and film reviews should vary from 500 to 1,000 words in length. The General Editor welcomes inquiries (by e-mail or telephone) prior to submission, regarding the suitability of works, stylistic questions, and so forth.

A Style Guide is available to authors upon request from the General Editor, and can be accessed from the Sehnsucht website. All works of any nature should conform to *Sehnsucht's* house style at the time of submission. Submissions that are not in stylistic conformity will be returned to the author for revision prior to evaluation.

Articles and reviews are evaluated as quickly as possible after submission. We endeavor to report back to the author(s) on the status of his/her submission within a reasonable time and without unnecessary delay. Ideally, notification of acceptance/rejection of a submitted work should occur within six weeks, though delays in this process occur from time to time.

The journal is committed to the pursuit of the highest of academic standards and to the pursuit of truth. For this reason, authors should be prepared to accept constructive criticism of their work even if they are experienced writers. We encourage both traditional and more contemporary approaches to the study of Lewis, including diverse (and emerging) methodologies. The journal is also committed to the advancement of the principles of mere Christianity as articulated by Lewis. All submissions will be evaluated in light of these considerations.

General inquiries should be made to the General Editor by e-mail (Bruce@scottsdalechurch.com) or telephone (480-998-1085). Submission of articles or reviews should be made by e-mail attachment in Word format; a hard copy should be retained by the author(s). To facilitate anonymity, the author's name and institutional affiliation should not appear in the article or review. Illustrations can be included, but it is the responsibility of the author(s) to provide a high quality impression (not a photocopy) and to secure copyright permission.

A full, detailed, style guide to which all submissions must conform follows.

Sehnsucht: The C. S. Lewis Journal
Style Guide

Introduction. Questions regarding stylistic issues should be addressed to the General Editor (bruce@scottsdalechurch.com) or to the Review Editor (thatlewislady@gmail.com) as early in the writing/submission process as possible.

I. General Instructions

1. Use 12 point type, double spaced.
2. Use Times New Roman font throughout (except for quotations from material originally written in non-Latin script). Use as little formatting as possible (only italics and capitalization where appropriate).
3. Use letter (or A4 for UK submissions) format with 1-inch margins.
4. When writing Lewis's full name, insert a space between initials (thus, C. S. Lewis). Employ the same form in similar cases.
5. Avoid the use of first person singular (except where it appears in quotations) whenever possible.
6. Place all tables at the end of the document, unless their insertion at an earlier location is regarded as essential.
7. Foreign words are to appear in italics.
8. Titles of books are to appear in italics; titles of books within titles are to be underlined.
9. Page numbers to be placed at top of page, center (in the header). Omit the page number on the first page.
10. Use American spellings, except in quotations where the original spellings should be preserved.
11. Ellipses, with spaces between the periods, should be used to indicate

all omissions in quotations.
12. To emphasize a word or term, use italic font, not bold.
13. Standardize all dates as follows:
    - 3 May 1993 (not May 3, 1993).
    - 1992-3 (not 1992-93).
14. Numbering:
    - Use Arabic (not Roman) numerals throughout (including biblical references).
    - Write out numbers in the text, except when referring to page numbers or dates ("sixteen were in attendance").
    - In footnotes, or when referring to page numbers, use 15-17 and 115-17 (for numbers in the teens).
    - However, for numbers in the twenties and beyond, use 21-3 (not 21-23) and 131-9 (not 131-39).
    - Avoid "f" or "ff"; instead list the entire range of numbers being cited, 45-6 (not 45f) and 45-51 (not 45ff).
15. Avoid use of the following abbreviations: "e.g.", "i.e.", "Cf.", "Ibid.", "idem.", "eidem", "et al.", "intro", "p.", "pp.", "f.", "ff.", and "&".
16. Incorporate the following abbreviations (in footnotes only): "MS", "vol.", "vols.", "ed.", "eds.", "trans.", "§".
17. For possessive form, use "Lewis's", not "Lewis'".
18. Insert a single space following a period (or full stop).
19. Do not insert a double space between paragraphs; instead, indent the first line of each new paragraph five (.5) spaces.
20. Avoid contractions (unless they appear from source material being quoted).
21. Use "(emphasis added)." at the end of the footnote when appropriate.
22. Use "premodernism"/ "postmodernism" (avoiding the hyphens).
23. Use the em-dash without spaces (aa—aa) only for interjections of material not subordinate to the main clause.
24. Christian/first name (or initials) of a person is to be used in the initial citation; surname/last name only used in all subsequent citations.
25. Follow the following rules for capitalization:
    - Capitalize the first word of a sentence and all proper names/nouns.

- Use H̲ell and H̲eaven (as per Lewis).
- Use B̲ible; b̲iblical; S̲cripture; G̲ospel(s).
- Use C̲hurch of England; Methodist C̲hurch; R̲oman C̲atholic C̲hurch; c̲hurch.
- Use I̲ncarnation, R̲esurrection, P̲atristic, A̲postolic, T̲rinity.
- Use *T̲he Chronicles of Narnia* (full title); t̲he *Chronicles* (short title).

26. The insertion of sections/subsections should be avoided in the body of the article.
27. Submit any images or charts in separate files with instructions in the text regarding where these elements should be placed.

II. Quotations

1. Periods/full stops should be placed *inside* the quotation mark (American style). Semi-colons should be placed outside the quotation marks.
2. Run-in quotations: quotations less than 45 words in length should be run into the text. Use double quotation marks. Use single quotation marks for a quotation that appears inside the quotation.
3. Block quotations: quotations of 45 words in length and longer should be set off from the text, single-spaced, each line indented .5 from the left-hand margin, without quotation marks (unless a quotation has been incorporated in the quotation, in which case single quotation marks are to be used), and in 12-point font. Double space between paragraphs. Do not indent the first sentence of a paragraph.

III. Footnotes

1. Use footnotes, not endnotes.
2. Use Times New Roman font, 10 point, single-spacing, first line indented .5.
3. List the first (Christian) name followed by last name (surname) of the author or editor, followed by a comma, book title (in italics; if an article is being cited, place the title in quotation marks), followed by a beginning parenthesis mark with the place of publication (followed by a colon), the publisher, (followed by a comma) and date of publication, followed by an end parenthesis mark, followed by a comma, followed by the page number(s).

4. Omit "p." and "pp." when indicating page number(s).
5. Do not insert an extra space between footnotes.
6. Avoid the use of "Ibid" or "Cf".
7. When multiple (but separate) quotations from a single source appear in the same sentence, only one footnote, inserted at the end of the sentence, is required.
8. Short title: After the initial citation of a work, use short title form on *all* subsequent citations.
9. Examples:
    i. **Books:**
        - Single author: Wesley A. Kort, *Reading C. S. Lewis: A Commentary* (New York: Oxford University Press, 2016), 166.
        - Multiple authors: David O'Hara and Matthew Dickerson, *Narnia and the Fields of Arbol: The Environmental Vision of C. S. Lewis* (Lexington, Kentucky: University Press of Kentucky, 2009), 22.
        - Editor: David Graham, ed., *We Remember C. S. Lewis* (Nashville: Broadman and Holman, 2001), ix.
        - Editor and translator: Norah Kershaw, ed. and trans., *Anglo-Saxon and Norse Poems* (Cambridge: Cambridge University Press, 1922), 60-3.
        - Multiple editors: Robert MacSwain and Michael Ward, eds., *The Cambridge Companion to C. S. Lewis* (Cambridge: Cambridge University Press, 2010), 6-7.
    ii. **Letters:** Letter of 24 May 1919, in C. S. Lewis, *The Collected Letters of C. S. Lewis*, ed. by Walter Hooper, 3 vols. (San Francisco: HarperCollins, 2004-7), 1:46.
    iii. **Published Diary:** Entry of 17 and 23 May 1922, in C. S. Lewis, *All My Road Before Me: The Diary of C. S. Lewis; 1922-1927*, ed. by Walter Hooper (San Diego: Harcourt Brace Jovanovich, 1991), 36, 39.
    iv. **Multi-volume work:** Paul Brazier, *C. S. Lewis: Revelation and the Christ*, 4 vols. (Eugene, Oregon: Wipf and Stock, 2012-14).
    v. **Journal Article:** Nancey Murphy, "Philosophical Resources for Postmodern Evangelical Theology," in *Christian Scholar's Review*, 26.2 (1996), 205.

vi. **Manuscript:** Charles J. F. Gilmore, MS *Royal Air Force Operations Record Book, Form 540, R.A.F. Chaplains' School, Cambridge,* AIR 29/752, April 1944, National Archives, Kew, 1.

vii. **Newspapers:** C. S. Lewis, "Professor Tolkien's Hobbit," Review of J. R. R. Tolkien, *The Hobbit: or There and Back Again,* in *The Times,* 2 October 1937, 714.

viii. **Chapters in Books:** Charles Gilmore, "To the RAF," in *C. S. Lewis at the Breakfast Table,* ed. by James T. Como (New York: Macmillan, 1979), 188.

ix. **Essays by C. S. Lewis within a Collection:** C. S. Lewis, "De Descriptione Temporum," in *Selected Literary Essays,* ed. by Walter Hooper (Cambridge: Cambridge University Press, 2013), 1-14.

x. **Internet Source:** www.narniaworld.com

xi. **Video/DVD:** C. S. Lewis, *The Chronicles of Narnia,* DVD (London: BBC Productions, 1990).

xii. **Short-title form:**
- Kort, *Reading C. S. Lewis,* 166.
- Letter of 26 August 1940, in Lewis, *CL,* 2:345.
- Entry of 17 May 1922, in Lewis, *All My Road,* 36.
- Murphy, "Philosophical Resources," 205.

IV. **Bibliography**
1. A separate bibliography is not required. When submitting a work that is bibliographical in nature, however, the following guidelines should be followed.
2. List the last name (surname) followed by first (Christian) name of the author or editor, followed by a period/full stop, title (in italics), etc.
3. Include the place of publication, publisher and date.
4. Use 10-point type and single space. Double space between entries.
5. Examples:
   i. Books:
   - Single author: Kort, Wesley A. *Reading C. S. Lewis: A Commentary.* New York: Oxford University Press, 2016.
   - Multiple authors: O'Hara, David and Matthew Dickerson. *Narnia and the Fields of Arbol: The Environmental Vision of*

C. S. Lewis. Lexington, Kentucky: University Press of Kentucky, 2009.
- Editor: Graham, David, ed. *We Remember C. S. Lewis*. Nashville: Broadman and Holman, 2001.
- Multiple editors: MacSwain, Robert and Michael Ward, eds. *The Cambridge Companion to C. S. Lewis*. Cambridge: University Press, 2010.

ii. **Letters:** Lewis, C. S. *The Collected Letters of C. S. Lewis*, ed. by Walter Hooper, 3 vols., San Francisco: HarperCollins, 2004-7.

iii. **Diary:** Lewis, C. S. *All My Road Before Me: The Diary of C. S. Lewis; 1922-1927*, ed. by Walter Hooper. San Diego: Harcourt Brace Jovanovich, 1991.

iv. **Multi-volume work:** Brazier, Paul. *C. S. Lewis: Revelation and the Christ*. Eugene, Oregon: Wipf and Stock, 2012-14.

v. **Journal Article:** Murphy, Nancey. "Philosophical Resources for Postmodern Evangelical Theology." *Christian Scholar's Review*, 26.2, 1996, 184-205.

vi. **Manuscript:** Gilmore, Charles J. F. MS *Royal Air Force Operations Record Book, Form 540, R.A.F. Chaplains' School, Cambridge*, AIR 29/752, April 1944. National Archives, Kew.

vii. **Newspapers:** Lewis, C. S. "Professor Tolkien's Hobbit," Review of J. R. R. Tolkien, *The Hobbit: or There and Back Again*," *The Times*, 2 October 1937, 714.

viii. **Internet source:** www.narniaworld.com

ix. **DVD/Video:** Lewis, C. S. *The Chronicles of Narnia*. DVD. London: BBC Production, 1990.

V. **Book Reviews/Film and Play Reviews**
  1. A book review should not attempt to summarize the content of the volume under review. Instead, it should aim to identify a book's principal argument(s) and its anticipated readership; evaluate its use of sources (both primary and secondary); situate the work in its field of scholarship (including the broad trends, biases, and assumptions of that field); and assess its overall contribution, including contemporary relevance.
  2. Although book reviews in *Sehnsucht* aim to be scholarly, clarity is more important than intellectual posturing. Attention should be

paid to simplicity of syntax and precision of meaning. A straight-forward recommendation or censure of the volume under review is encouraged.
3. The length of a review is between 500 and 1000 words, except in exceptional circumstances when the quality or importance of a volume justifies a lengthier review. If it is anticipated that a review is to exceed this length, prior consultation with the Review Editor (thatlewislady@gmail.com) is essential.
4. Volumes of particular importance or interest may be allowed greater consideration. In some cases, the Book Review Editor will assign a work to be covered in a Review Essay, which may run up to 5,000 words in length.
5. Reviews should begin (written in single space) with author's/editor's name(s), full title, place and date of publication (in parenthesis), the number of pages, the price (in US dollars), and the 13-digit ISBN (omitting the hyphens).
6. The number of pages should include the preface (in Roman numerals), index, appendices, notes, and index. The inclusion of graphs and illustrations (if any) should also be noted. Example: Michael Ward, *The Narnia Code: C. S. Lewis and the Secret of the Seven Heavens* (Carol Stream, Illinois: Tyndale House, 2010). 193 pages, including "For Further Reading" and Discussion Guide. $13.99. ISBN 9781414339658.
7. The body of the review should be typed, double-spaced, and in conformity to the style guidelines outlined above.
8. All quotations and direct references must be followed by the page number (in parenthesis) of the text in which they appear and preceding punctuation marks. The exception is in indented, long quotations where the page number (in parenthesis) follows the ending period.
9. The name of the author of the review, together with his/her place of academic affiliation (or residence) should be provided at the end of the review, written in single space on the left margin.
10. Examples
    i. **Book Review:** Janice Brown, *The Lion in the Waste Land: Fearsome Redemption in the Work of C. S. Lewis, Dorothy L. Sayers,*

and T. S. Eliot (Kent, OH: Kent State University Press, 2018). xiv + 290 pages. $45.00. ISBN 9781606353387.

ii. **DVD/Video/CD Review:** Paul McCusker, *C. S. Lewis at War: The Dramatic Story Behind Mere Christianity* (Carol Stream, IL: Tyndale House, 2014). 8 audio CDs. $39.99. ISBN 9781624052187.

iii. **Theater Review:** *The Horse and His Boy*, based on the book by C. S. Lewis, adapted by Nicole Stratton, starring Isaiah Johnson, Hope Barr, Micah Hamilton, and Sheri Chavers. Taylors, SC: The Logos Theatre, 1 March 2019.

iv. **Film Review:** *Tolkien*, by David Gleeson and Stephen Beresford, directed by Dome Karukoski, starring Nicholas Hoult and Lily Collins. Century City, CA: Fox Searchlight, 2019.

30 November 2020

Copyright

Unless otherwise noted, the copyright of all material published in *Sehnsucht: The C. S. Lewis Journal* is held by the Arizona C. S. Lewis Society. Permission to quote from this material in works of scholarship is granted on the understanding that full citation (e.g., name of author, full title, name of article/review, name of journal, page number, etc.) will be provided, and on the understanding that no financial gain or profit will accrue to the author. Permission to photocopy this material is granted to individuals for the purpose of internal or personal use only. For all other uses, permission in writing must be obtained from the Arizona C. S. Lewis Society.

Sehnsucht: The C. S. Lewis Journal
Subscription Form

Volume 17: 2023

Please photocopy this form and send it with your payment to:

The Arizona C. S. Lewis Society
c/o 29217 N. 70th Avenue
Peoria, Arizona 85383

Make subscription checks payable to
"Arizona C. S. Lewis Society"
Annual Price: $25; Institutions $30

NAME: _____

ADDRESS:_____

_____

NAME ON CARD: _____

CREDIT CARD TYPE (M/C, VISA, AMEX)_____

CARD NUMBER: _____

EXPIRATION DATE: _____

SIGNATURE: _____

TODAY'S DATE: _____

All past volumes of *Sehnsucht* are available as print-on-demand versions through Wipf and Stock Publishers, https://wipfandstock.com.

Volume 1 (2007)
Volume 2 (2008)
Volume 3 (2009)
Volumes 5/6 (2011-12) – double volume
Volumes 7/8 (2013-14) – double volume
Volume 9 (2015)
Volume 10 (2016)
Volume 11 (2017)
Volume 12 (2018)
Volume 13 (2019)
Volume 14 (2020)
Volume 15 (2021)
Volume 16 (2022)

www.ingramcontent.com/pod-product-compliance
Lightning Source LLC
Chambersburg PA
CBHW070918180426
43192CB00038B/1773